YOUR CHURCH N

*Rediscover the Transformative Power
of Serving Together*

Updated Second Edition of
Heroic Church Membership

ISBN 979-8-9881279-6-3

Emissary
PUBLISHING

Published in Phoenix, Arizona by Emissary Publishing.
Emissary is a business trade name of Ed's Voices, LLC.

Scripture quotations are taken from the King James Bible,
unless otherwise cited/specified.

DEDICATION

This effort is dedicated unto the God who loved me and
gave himself for me at Calvary.

And to my wife, Karla, who has loved me unceasingly, believed in me
unwaveringly, and followed me unselfishly. She is my heart and my
biggest fan. She has always encouraged me to write.

"Hey Karla, I did it!"

Praise For "Your Church Needs You"

One of the most effective methods used to influence the thinking and beliefs of others is personal testimony. God showed the Apostle Paul this method in Acts 22:15 and Paul used it many times but especially before Agrippa the King in Acts 26:12-20. Pastor Cory Sexton has employed this method in "Your Church Needs You." He provides an honest and straight forward account of his own journey as a saved and yet struggling Christian in understanding what involvement, responsibility and dedication was required in becoming a church member. In this manual of instruction about what true church membership should look like, we are provided with a clear picture of the spiritual temperature of the average church and its lack of orienting and nurturing the new member to his/her participation in the life of the body. If we should take a survey in today's modern church world, I think we would find a great vacuum existing in the believer. Many know that they are saved but haven't a clue as to what true church membership is all about. "Your Church Needs You" could not have come at a more needed time. In it, Pastor Sexton addresses the issues confronting the church and its members in a loving, truthful, and encouraging way. I personally believe if this practical manual could find its way into the hands of Pastors, then to their membership and was implemented, it would be used by God to take us back to a Biblical understanding of what the first church practiced as they "continued steadfastly in the apostle's doctrine and fellowship, and in breaking of bread and in prayers". In this treaty we see God's wonderful grace in the lives of two people who gave themselves to be faithful to the Lord. Then we are introduced to "typical and atypical" church membership. He then ushers us on to doctrinally sound instruction regarding "sacrificial selflessness and service", and then to the stewardship of the believer as it relates to the financial needs of the local church and how each member can serve. My prayer is that our great God will see fit to cause this book to be widely distributed and used by all local churches.

Gary Deems, D. Min. Th.D. Ph. D.

Pastor Sexton has given us something we have needed a long time: a brief, well-reasoned explanation of what sets the great church member apart. His prescription for anemic Christianity, heroic sacrifice, is the polar opposite of the me-centered Christianity so prevalent in our day. Sacrifice has always been the hallmark of heroism, but it has seldom been applied to church membership in such a clear and undeniable way. I say undeniable because of the abundance of Scripture given to substantiate each point. This is not a man's opinion piece – it is a practical explanation of basic Bible Christianity.

Potential uses are limitless. It could be placed into the hands of a new convert, studied in a new-members class, or given to the person who asks, "What does God want me to do?" The first answer to that question is: "Become an uncommon church member." The disciplines, experience and Spirituality that would be developed by that focus would cause God's churches to flourish as well as provide practical basic training for those called into wider fields of service. Written by a man on the front lines of God's work, this book explains it all!

Tom Miles, Retired Church Pastor - 54 years in the Ministry
Senior Pastor, Crooked Creek Baptist Church, 29 years and 5 months

We are told in First Kings 14:25-26 that Shishak, king of Egypt, took away the treasures of the house of the Lord. Pastor Cory Sexton, in this book, "Your Church Needs You," clearly unveils for us the treasures that the god of this world, Satan, has taken away from the church, the House of the Lord. In my more than fifty years of being a Christian I don't believe I have ever read anything that even comes close to pinpointing the problems with the church membership of today as this book. I will not list those treasures here, but I highly recommend that you get a copy of this book and see for yourself the things that are missing in our churches today. I believe you will be as intrigued, convicted, challenged, and enlightened as I was. Thank you, Pastor Sexton.

Dr. Jack L. Lawson, Pastor Emeritus
Jackson County Baptist Church

Jesus loves the church! Any doubt about our Lord's affection for His Body, the church, is laid to rest when we read the words "Christ also loved the church, and gave himself for it;" – Ephesians 5:25b. In his book, "Your Church Needs You," Pastor Cory Sexton implores church members to love what Jesus loved and sacrifice for what Jesus sacrificed for – His Church.

In a day when professing Christians are searching for the most convenient option to check off the church box, Cory Sexton pleads with them to look at church from a different perspective. Sexton reminds his reader that the church is not a place for consumers but for contributors. He reminds us that ordinary church ministry is extraordinary when it's done with a sacrificial and Christ-honoring spirit.

If you would like to know what Biblical, Christ-honoring, eternity-impacting church membership looks like, this book is a must-read! Pastors and ministry leaders will benefit from reading this material and passing it on to their congregants. Together, church leaders and laity can use this book to recapture a Scriptural vision for Christ's love—the local church.

Stephen Burrell, Pastor
Faith Baptist Church. Jefferson, Georgia.

It was a blessing to read this book. Pastor Sexton certainly put into words what many pastors are seeing and feeling in their own churches. Even on the mission field, we have seen and heard for ourselves the lack of understanding of what a church member should look like. This wonderful book, "Your Church Needs You," clearly and biblically answers those questions for anyone looking to understand what their role is in the local church. In a day and age where the average churchgoer gets caught up and lost in a multi-campus mega-church growth movement, and the pastoral teams are losing touch with the membership, Brother Cory does a tremendous job of laying out biblical doctrine and practical theology of the local church. He clearly shows how, through a lack of biblical understanding and commitment to one's local church, the family and community are affected to their detriment.

Brother Cory, thank you for your pastor's heart for your people and for the local church. My prayer is that God will use this book to stir hearts to the point that each reader will see his or her need to be the member God has called them to be, all for the furtherance of the gospel, the edification of the body of Christ, and ultimately to the Glory of God!

Missionary Jason Hamby

Far North Director, Macedonia World Baptist Missions Inc.

The local church is the agent by which God primarily works today. Workers are raised through the local church, and the Gospel is proclaimed from the local church. Every child of God should belong to a local church.

Pastor Cory uses Biblical truth and personal experience to speak on this vital subject of church membership. My prayer, along with that of Pastor Cory, is that every Christian would become a heroic member of their church!

Jeffrey Bush

Vision Baptist Missions, President

Few things are needed any more today than for Christians to take church membership seriously. Cory Sexton has written an excellent book on that very subject. Based on his own personal journey, along with his many years of experience as a pastor, Sexton's book is a welcome tonic for what ails many Christians: an anemic church membership. The combination of practical help and personal presentation makes for interesting reading. Not only should church members take church membership seriously, but so should pastors, according to Sexton! Whether you are a pastor or a church member,

"Your church needs you, sacrificially!" This book tells you how to do that.

Dr. David L. Allen

Distinguished Professor of Practical Theology
Dean, Adrian Rogers Center for Biblical Preaching
Mid-America Baptist Theological Seminary

Table of Contents

Foreword

Our society is more connected than any previous generation before us. Social media unites us with friends we've never seen, followers we've never known, and family we've never met. We know what people eat, where they take vacations when they change jobs, and how they feel about certain political situations based on a digitalized thumbs-up and thumbs-down system. In this viral age, it is possible to process a lot of information about others without ever really knowing them on a personal and intimate level.

Granted, such connectivity is convenient, easy, and the way of the world; however, it tends to create superficial (perhaps even artificial) relationships. As virtual interaction becomes the normative means of communication in our culture, the more detached we become from real, meaningful engagement.

God designed the church to be something altogether different.

Although technology has been and can be a tool for church ministry, it cannot be a substitute for the actual church itself. By sheer virtue of our name, the church is the assembly. It is the calling out and the coming together of believers in a local community who unite their faith, their lives, their attendance, and their gospel efforts for the glory of God. Like a natural body, the church has many parts and many members that exist together in a harmonious and synchronized fashion. A body part that is isolated from the whole quickly loses its life and vitality. Even so, it is impossible to *be* the church without *being part* of the church, the Body of Christ.

In the pages ahead, Pastor Cory Sexton does a remarkable job of detailing the privileges and responsibilities of being part of the local church. He not only accentuates the scriptural mandates of church membership, but he calls upon each believer to take their involvement, their spiritual giftedness, and their covenantal obligations of the assembly seriously. In *Your Church Needs You*, you will be challenged, admonished, and greatly encouraged to take ownership of your membership. This is a great and timely read for our remotely engaged generation.

Kenneth Kuykendall

Acknowledgments

Aesop states, "A man is known by the company he keeps." The Psalmist says, "Blessed is the man that walketh not in the counsel of the ungodly, nor standeth in the way of sinners, nor sitteth in the seat of the scornful." The Proverbs state, "He that walketh with wise men shall be wise: but a companion of fools shall be destroyed." I Have been blessed by some good company. I say blessed not just because of the character of the men I have known but because God superintended my steps so that I would be exposed to such men in the first place.

I am thankful for these men, and there are too many to list, but they have helped me, trained me, pushed me to be better, and challenged me to study more. Now, I see that any wisdom I possess has been handed down to me from other men whom I have had the pleasure of working under and learning from.

Of course, the first such man was my father. My father invested an inordinate amount of time and energy in me, and because of it, we have become friends first and foremost. I have sought to do likewise with my own children. My mother has doted upon me and has always made me feel special. For these two, I am most thankful, and I seek to honor them with my life.

Second only to my Salvation, the greatest gift God has ever given me is my dear wife and our precious children. My greatest joys are found in my family. I have truly loved being a husband and a father. We are a unit; nothing comes between us; we are built to last. I seek to make you guys proud with my every effort.

Lastly, to the congregation at Hoschton Baptist Church, thank you for allowing me to be your Pastor and Shepherd. I sincerely pray that the Lord will allow us to finish what we have started together. Special Thanks to Leila Scoggins for her editorial and design work. She is a trooper and has been a tremendous help in this project.

Introduction

I have had the dream of writing a book for several years, but every time I set out to do so, the pragmatist in me takes over. I decide that the subject upon which I desire to write is either too well covered by current materials or that someone else is much more qualified for the work, and so I leave off writing even before I begin.

I am not at all sure that this subject is any different, as it is likely well-covered. I am certain that there are other authors, pastors, and professors who are more qualified to address this material than I am. However, I am writing this with a burden and a belief that my testimony and experience are viable. I believe that they can be viewed as exemplary by others.

Exactly why am I writing this? Simply put, because I see a need. There is a need among all churches for workers, dedicated workers, committed servants of God who faithfully work throughout their salvation with fear and trembling, knowing that it is God who works within them to accomplish His good will in their lives (Philippians 2:12-13). This need is among all churches, but it is more evident among smaller churches, whether new or old, young or aged, a fresh church plant or a struggling church revitalization project. Dedicated, driven, and devoted workers are often very difficult to find and equally difficult to develop.

I have had experience in several church environments and the common denominator in all of them is the need for sincere and faithful workers. Obviously, relief comes with numbers.

The larger the congregation, typically the greater the available workforce, but from my experience, the quality (dedication, devotion, sincerity, drive, and faithfulness) is not automatically affected by the quantity. While I do not mean to be hyperbolic, and I certainly have no desire to appear defeated, this need is crippling to many causes, and a great number of ministries suffer because of a lack of willing and able workers.

I am a pastor. I believe that when God called me, he began a process in my heart, and that process has helped me love people. This love causes me to believe in people. I believe that people want to do right. I believe that born-again people desire to do right in the eyes of the Lord, as is relative to the Word of God and in relation to the House of God and the Body of Christ. I sincerely believe that folks want to serve in the Church, they want to help the pastor, they want to win the community, they want to do all the things that seem fitting for the Body of Christ, but they simply don't know how, and they have become convinced that they can never really know how. So, they are happy to let the pastor and his staff, if he is blessed to have one, do the work. I believe the truths contained in Ephesians 4, God has given to the church every gift that is necessary for success and wellbeing.

Furthermore, I am a work of grace. I know what God did in my heart, and likewise in the heart of my wife, and how it totally transformed our Church experience and involvement. I am not speaking of our salvation experience; rather, I am referring to the moment in which we surrendered our lives and the lives of our children unto the Lord and His service in the Church, which is the Body of Christ, for whom He gave His life.

And before you turn me off, this surrender occurred at the end of a decade of backsliding and two full years before ministry became a calling in our lives. When we surrendered it was to be dedicated, devoted, attending church members. Therefore, I believe that there are many who could and would experience this same transformation if they understood its implications. It is my desire to reveal what that means to me in the following pages. I pray that you will receive it and that the Lord will benefit you in the process.

E. Cory Sexton

Chapter One
A Testimony of God's Grace in Salvation

It may not be completely customary for an author to share his salvation story in full while writing about active, meaningful church membership, but that is what I am going to do.

My testimony begins like many "church kid" testimonies. I was raised by godly, churchgoing, church-serving parents. In fact, my father was a preacher. Are you shocked? Of course not, because this is a very familiar testimony. Allow me to personalize it moving forward.

My mother and father were married in 1967. He was 28, and she was 24; it was their second marriage. He was the father of five children – three girls and two boys. She was the mother of two children, both boys. They had both experienced a very difficult first marriage, complicated by youth and poverty. I was born in 1968 to complete the package. You might say that we were the original Brady Bunch, although I am quite sure there were many others.

At the time of their marriage, they were not attending church together; in fact, my father was not even a believer. My mother had come to faith as a young girl of 8 years old under the ministry of Dr. Curtis Hutson, and she continued to attend church as a young lady and throughout her young life. Once they were married, she still attended a local church along with all the children. In 1969, my father accepted the Lord as his Savior; he later surrendered to preach and attended Immanuel Bible College from 1972 to 1976, graduating with a bachelor's degree in biblical studies.

To see them today, you would never know the difficulties that they have faced. And I must say, with a tear, that much of their difficulties came at the hands of well-meaning yet uncompassionate pastors. This book is certainly not intended for that discussion. I am simply stating that these events have affected me, shaped me even. Today, my folks have been married for 54 years. They have eight children, six sons and daughters-in-love, 20 plus grandchildren, 20 plus great-grandchildren, and several great-great grandchildren. They are blessed and favored by the Lord.

Growing up, we attended church regularly. You've heard about the kids with "drug problems... whose parents drug them to church every time the doors were opened?" Well, that was me, or I should say us. We never wondered if we were going to church. And that included Sunday morning, Sunday evening, Wednesday evening, and any other time that the church we were attending had service. If the church was meeting, we were attending. That was life.

We moved around a bit; my father had great teaching ability, and he wanted to do so much more, so we moved often, looking for a church that could and would use him. There was never a shortage of teaching and even preaching opportunities because he was gifted, and someone was always looking for help. He would undertake prison ministries, nursing home ministries, youth ministries, and Sunday school ministries, but there was always unrest as he struggled to deal with the status quo. This would also affect me.

Over the years, I have had a great affinity for several pastors. I will not name them for fear of leaving someone out, but many of my childhood memories revolve around church, Sunday School teachers, pastors, and evangelists. I was a "typical" church kid.

In 1979 at 11 years old, I spent several Sunday evenings at the altar of a new church plant that we were attending. The pastor was young, he had a great evangelistic zeal, and I had a connection with him.

Many times that summer, he would pray with me, and when we finished praying, he would say, "You're Safe," and I would say, "Does that mean I am saved?" And he would say, "No, son, but you're safe." I have always appreciated the fact that he did not rush me; he knew I needed to mature more in my understanding. Eventually, that summer, I would make a profession of faith, and he would baptize me, and so I would approach my teen years with some semblance of faith.

By the mid-1980s, the burdens and hurts of the ministry overcame my parents' zeal to serve; they had simply been hurt too much.

So, their dedication to attending began to wane, and shortly thereafter, they stopped attending at all. Again, I am not here to argue this; rather, I am telling my salvation story, which includes the events that the Lord used to mold me.

This occurrence in my parents' lives coincided with my teen years. While we were attending church at another relatively new church plant with another tremendous pastor, whom I loved, I would participate in the youth group, sing in the youth choir, and attend Sunday School. Again, I would say that I was the "average" church kid.

But away from church, I was not doing well at all. I had developed an angry spirit, I had become averse to almost any authority, including my parents but most especially the authority at school. I had developed some pretty bad habits, and I was drifting from any real belief in the Lord, or the Bible, or the need to attend church. And as he always does, Satan was sure to supply the circumstances and friends that I needed to be carried even farther than I desired. This period of my life would culminate with me leaving high school on the first day of my senior year without graduating and casting myself headlong into an independent, rebellious, self-serving lifestyle.

I went on to attend a technical school, graduate, and become a certified automotive technician. All the while, I was developing the new, rebellious, independent spirit that I would struggle with for the next decade or more. Soon after graduating, and with my father's help, I would open a repair facility of my own; I was only 20 years old, I was a gifted technician, and I was the boss. My disdain for authority was nearly complete, and my desires now turned almost wholly to wealth and the acquisition of it. I wanted to be successful. I wanted to be the best. I wanted to be respected, and I wanted it badly.

That 11-year-old kid who loved church, pastors, and Sunday School teachers and whom the pastor said was safe wasn't so safe anymore. Indeed, I was lost, having never truly accepted the Lord as my Savior. I had professed salvation but never possessed it.

In the spring of 1989, at the age of 21. I began to feel some things that I had not felt before. One day, while at work, I became convinced that I would soon die and likely go to Hell. I became literally terrified, I could not wait any longer, so I called the last pastor that I had known. He invited me to his office; it was a Tuesday afternoon in May.

After some discussion and a reminder of things that I had well known before, I determined that I had never truly repented of my unbelief; I had never received Christ as my Savior and Lord. I was at war, and in my opinion, the war would soon end, and Hell would be my destination.

There, in the pastor's office, under the conviction of the Holy Spirit of God, I knelt and begged for forgiveness, and the Lord saved me. My heart changed. I was no longer angry. I was no longer resistant to apparent authorities; I was at peace. Jesus was Lord, and He had saved me. I attended that church the following Sunday and was baptized, this time with a clear understanding of what was happening.

And as sure as I am speaking today, my intentions were to attend church, and to serve the Lord, and to help that pastor, but I did not...

All too soon, I was too busy to attend. I was working long hours and had little time off, so church would just have to wait.

In December of 1990, I married my eighth-grade sweetheart. We had dated on and off for several years, and finally, the Lord allowed us to marry. Karla was born and raised in Dacula, Georgia, and had attended Dacula First Baptist most of her life. She had a great pastor, and she had enjoyed her time growing up in church: singing in the choir, participating with the youth group, etc. Karla was saved at a tent revival when she was 12, and she was comfortable with the idea of attending and serving in the church.

When we married, I would say that we had intentions of attending church. We were not living a righteous life, but we were certainly not anti-church, anti-religious gatherings or anti-God. However, there were just too many excuses.

In December 1993, we had our first child, a sweet little baby girl. During the pregnancy, we often spoke about needing to find a church and how we would as soon as she was born. We did not...

In June 1998, we had our second child, a handsome little baby boy. We had attempted church a time or two with Kayla, our daughter, but just couldn't find that "perfect" church. When we discovered that Carter was on the way, we once again spoke about finding a church home, but we would wait until he was born before looking further.

During the first eight years of our marriage, we enjoyed much success. We were financially comfortable. We both had rewarding careers. We had most anything that we wanted. We did not suffer much loss or sadness. Life was good. This led to arrogance on my part. I was so confident that these things were all my doing or our doing that I would regularly chide anyone who complained about difficulty, stress, or failure.

But around my 30th birthday, I began to experience some unsettling thoughts and emotions. I shared these with some men in my life and received some pretty terrible advice. Some of the advice is too awful to share, but many assumed that I was experiencing a midlife crisis. At 30 years old!? One suggested that I buy a Harley, another suggested that I develop a hobby (one that did not include my wife), and others suggested that I double down on my career.

While I was receiving this stellar advice, I tried several things on my own. I quit my job, then quit another job, and bought a bigger truck… but none of these things helped.

I'd been married for ten years, had two children ages 5 and 1, had a wonderful relationship with my wife, had career successes, was in good health, and lived a happy life, but something was missing. Finally, we began looking for a church. We thought this community involvement might be good, and the kids needed to grow up in church, so we set out to find the "perfect" church.

This would go on for a while. We tried a couple of churches, but it wasn't easy; we didn't really know what we were looking for, our parents were not in church at the time, and we didn't have church friends (in fact, we lost most of our friends when we started attending church). We tried a local, old, established church, but it was too stuffy. We tried a country church, but it was too small. We tried a contemporary church, but it was too modern. Then we would quit trying for a week or two. Then we thought we should try Sunday School and get to know people, but the first class we attended, they were talking about stress, and I had a pretty low (wrong) opinion of people who had stress problems. Unfortunately, they asked my opinion... and I think we are still banned from that Sunday School class.

In retrospect, I realize now that we really were not looking for a church. Instead, we were looking for a club or a medicine that would make us feel better, and we kept finding an excuse. Eventually, we determined to visit one more church. I had family there, so maybe this would be the one.

I remember very little about that church service. I don't remember the music. I don't remember who was sitting nearby. I don't even remember the message, the text, or the words the preacher spoke, but I do remember that they were all especially for me. I remember feeling inadequate, I remember feeling embarrassed, I remember feeling like I was on an island, and everyone was looking at me. I specifically remember thinking about how my folks had struggled for acceptance and how they fought to keep us in church until they couldn't bear the pain any longer.

I remember thinking of how God had blessed my life. He had given me a wife that I adored, healthy children that I loved, a career that I enjoyed, a house that I was proud of, and a life with very little struggle. And I had repaid Him by walking away, living for me, and promoting myself. I remember thinking how poorly I had turned out, and that was with a childhood in the church. What would my kids be like?

Karla and I enjoyed God's Grace in salvation, and we would soon enjoy God's grace in restoration.

Can I tell you now how desperately you need to be saved? Can I tell you how you will look for satisfaction and peace, but it cannot be found outside of a saving relationship with Jesus?

This is a diverse world, full of diverse people, all with one similarity, they are born sinners. We are all born in sin. We are all one race. We are humans, and we are all descendants of Adam. We are told in Romans 5:12, "Wherefore, as by one man sin entered into the world, and death by sin; and so death passed upon all men, for that all have sinned." We also see in Romans 3:23, "For all have sinned, and come short of the glory of God." And again, in Romans 6:23, "For the wages of sin is death; but the gift of God is eternal life through Jesus Christ our Lord."

So, we see that we have a common problem, sin and eventually death. There is also a common solution. John 3:16 says, "For God so loved the world, that he gave his only begotten Son, that whosoever believeth in him should not perish, but have everlasting life. " And again, we are told in Romans 10:9-13, "That if thou shalt confess with thy mouth the Lord Jesus, and shalt believe in thine heart that God hath raised him from the dead, thou shalt be saved. For with the heart man believeth unto righteousness; and with the mouth confession is made unto salvation. For the scripture saith, Whosoever believeth on him shall not be ashamed. For there is no difference between the Jew and the Greek: for the same Lord over all is rich unto all that call upon him. For whosoever shall call upon the name of the Lord shall be saved."

Would you come to Jesus today? Have you experienced the dissatisfaction of life without Him? Would you pray this prayer?

Father, I come humbly today seeking your forgiveness. I know that I am a sinner and realize that I am guilty of sin. God, I come today seeking the salvation that is only found in The Lord Jesus Christ. I have lived my life for me; I have been my own god, and lord, I repent of that sin of unbelief. I know that you are God, you are the creator, and you are the one in whom all things consist. I know that you paid my sin debt on the Cross of Calvary. I trust today, not in a prayer or a promise, but Lord in a person, you, and in a power, your finished work. Lord, thank you for saving me!

Chapter Two
A Testimony of God's Grace in Restoration

As we stood that morning during the invitation, listening to the pianist playing, and the pastor's imploring words, we stood together, and though I do not specifically remember, we were probably holding hands as we are accustomed to do. Also, the rest of the attendees were standing that morning, and again, I don't specifically remember, but the sanctuary there is large, so many other folks were standing all over the auditorium, but I felt as if I was standing all alone. As if it were just me and the Lord, standing, staring, and shamefully shaking.

He had saved me at great expense to himself, and though I was not clear on the details, I knew that it was a horrible, excruciating death. I knew He was God; I knew that everything I had was because He had granted it. I knew that there had to be some expectations of me. And I knew that I had in no way been faithful to fulfill those expectations.

I have always found it quite intriguing that we are not more in tune with the expectations. Surely you know what I mean. We live in a world of give and take. We are raised with the understanding that if someone does something for you, there are likely some expectations, and those expectations are usually standard as they center around gratitude and thanksgiving. Yet we often see someone accept the free gift of God's grace and abscond with it as if they earned it, stole it, or were deserving of it, without ever stopping to consider what the expectations are.

But I digress; I am back in that church, on that Sunday morning, standing on that island of guilt, wondering if the Lord would have me back, if he would forgive me for living selfishly, if he would restore the wasted years. And I came to another wrong conclusion. I decided that I was damaged goods, that God could not use me, that I had tarnished whatever was good about me … but that even if that was true, I would be faithful. I would bring my family to church. I would at least do that.

The next problem I had was Karla. We had not spoken yet (we were still in the church). What if I was the only one who felt so convicted, what if I was the only one who felt so obligated? What if she didn't like the church, what if she wouldn't come back to this church? My mind was spinning.

Once again, my memory for details is not that great. But I do remember where we were parked. I remember loading the kids up, and sitting in the car, so relieved to be out of that service. The emotions were so high, and I didn't want to embarrass myself. We sat there for what seemed to be a long time in my memory. I began to weep; I was so ashamed. I had led my family, but not to church. I had provided for my family, but not spiritually. I had loved my wife and kids but not the way a Christian father and husband should. And as I wept, she wept with me. We were on the same page, we felt the same conviction, we experienced the same guilt, and we made the same promise that no matter what, we would not miss any more church. We would be there every time the doors opened.

We were back that night and that Wednesday, and the next Sunday, we were in Sunday School. Before long, we joined the church, then the choir, began tithing, started reading the Bible at home, and tried to have family devotions.

We learned something at every service, made church friends, and attended church events. It was a whole new world, a restored position within the family of God, a place where we belonged.

We were well-dressed and well-mannered, so people thought we were church folks. They thought we just came from another church and became active in their church. I wish they had known what was really happening. It was amazing. So, quickly, God restored us to the family. And the only commitment that we made, the only one we were able to make, was a commitment to attend. I had nothing to offer the Lord except my attendance, and He said, "That'll do!"

Not long after we began attending church faithfully, I began to see what I had missed. The belonging, the participating, the corporate worship was like a salve to my soul. I wanted more, and I wanted to do more. But then I remembered that I was just damaged goods, and that God would not use me, so I would just be faithful and bring my kids. It wasn't a bad deal, I got to be there and worship and learn and grow. I got to sing in the choir, and sometimes a solo or a duet with Karla. I was just happy to be there.

Then, one day, I heard someone preaching on the Prodigal Son from Luke 15. This preacher brought it to my attention that this boy, this wayward one, this rebel was always a son. When he demanded that the father give him his portion, he was a son. When he went to the far country and squandered all his goods in riotous living, he was still a son. When he sold himself into service, he was still a son. When he was feeding those pigs, he was still a son, and the father was still waiting for his return.

And when he arose to return, filthy, and ragged, and destitute, and hungry, he was still a son. And when the father saw him "when he was yet a great way off." The father ran unto him and had compassion on him. And kissed him. And as that boy, that filthy, self-willed, defeated boy spoke and said, "I am no more worthy," the father said, "Bring forth the best robe. Bring him a ring. Put shoes on his feet. He is not a servant, he is not a slave, he is not unworthy. He is my son. He was dead and is alive again. He was lost but now is found."

The preacher explained how that robe was a picture of Christ's righteousness, in which we are robed. And that ring is a sign of adoption, it means that he is an adult son who can do business as a representative of the family. The shoes were to display his status as a free man because slaves did not have shoes. All the filth that boy got himself into while he was rebelling, the father covered with his own robe and then he restored the family privileges at once.

In that sermon the Lord taught me that I became His son, a Child of the King, way back in 1989. When I repented of my unbelief, he saved me and sealed me for time and eternity.

For some time, I was like that wayward son, but I was a son just the same. I had wasted ten plus years living riotously, squandered a lot of the gifts and abilities that God had given me, and done so in a far country in pursuit of mammon. But when I came back, by the grace of God, I did not come back as damaged goods because he could and would restore me.

We get a great representation of this truth in 1 John 1:9, "If we confess our sins, he is faithful and just to forgive us our sins, and to cleanse us from all unrighteousness." As we confess, He forgives and restores. Isn't that wonderful news? I had spent some wasteful years, but God was not finished with me, and now I knew that I had been restored. With this restoration came the freedom to become what God intended for me to be.

Let's take a moment to establish the timeline again because I do not want to mislead you, whether purposefully or accidentally. We began attending church faithfully in the spring of that year. When we started, we went from zero attendance to full attendance immediately. That was the only commitment that we believed we could make. Almost immediately, we started looking to see how we could help (because we believe that with all gifts come expectations). Before summer, we were regulars in the choir. We helped with VBS during the summer. In the fall, I was appointed as a Sunday School officer. During the winter, we were asked to take the middle school Sunday School class.

I am not sharing this timeline as a means of boasting. In fact, it is mostly from memory, and therefore, I could not prove it if I needed to. The point is not what we did; the point is *that* we did.

If you are reading this book, I am sure you are not reading to establish some sort of competition with me. If that is the case, I can recommend some better candidates for you to compete with. I hope that you are reading to discover what membership in a church is supposed to look like and possibly how you can attain it.

I am not presenting myself or my family as examples of church "heroes" either, but I am presenting us as examples of commitment because from the one commitment to be faithful to the church, the Lord has completely transformed my life, and I believe He will do the same for you (while at the same time benefiting the church you love).

I want to share this one more gift of God with you before we close this chapter. During our first two years of faithful church attendance, the Lord removed several things from our life. Things we thought we enjoyed and things we believed we could never live without. But one by one, he took away all the alcohol, and then he took away all the tobacco, and then he removed the secular and worldly music that was creating poor attitudes in our lives, he took away my desire for wealth, he took away my desire for notoriety. None of these things seemed to be a problem to me, but one by one, they became a hindrance to what the Lord was doing in my life and in Karla's life.

As he took those things, he began to give other things in their place: desires, gifts, dreams, and abilities. And they always complimented each other. I would develop this desire, and then the Lord would provide an opportunity for me to exercise the gift that would fulfill that desire.

It happened several times, and each one seemed a little grander than the last. Everything from singing, to playing the guitar, to teaching youth, to working in a Bible camp, and then eventually even preaching. I want to share my call to preach with you quickly, and then we will close this chapter.

I had begun teaching a seventh and eighth-grade Sunday School class. There were only about 10 students, but they were all church kids. I was super aware that they had some biblical knowledge, so I always prepared well because I didn't want to be embarrassed.

One evening I was studying in Isaiah 6 about the glory of the Lord. When I noticed that Isaiah responded to an open call. The Lord said, "Whom shall I send, and who will go for us?" And Isaiah said, "Here am I, send me!" I had been considering the call to preach, but as always, I dealt with an inferior feeling, but God reminded me that He had restored me. Then I wondered about the gifting, but God had enabled me to do other things. Then I worried about my family, and specifically Karla because she didn't marry a preacher and I didn't want to do anything to hurt her. And as I sat there that evening pondering these things, I heard a knock on my office door. When I looked up, it was Karla; she said, "I just want you to know that I've given you to the Lord, and whatever He calls you to do, I am with you."

Once again, God had given me the desire and the opportunity, and now, through my wife, He gave me the courage to announce my call to the church. I announced my call to preach to Faith Baptist Church in August 2002, roughly 18 months after committing to be faithful.

The title of this chapter is God's Grace in Restoration. That is exactly what I have experienced, and you can experience it as well. You may be in a far country, you may have drifted, you may have wandered, but you do not need to remain there one second longer. If you repent, He will restore.

He is faithful and just to forgive us from all unrighteousness. I wonder if you would stop reading and pray right now, just where you are and how you are?

God, I have wandered far but now I'm coming home. Father, I repent of those selfish days, those riotous nights. Lord, I am seeking restoration, and though I know I am unworthy if you will you can restore and make whole again all that I have wasted. Lord, I trust you and believe that you will restore and cleanse me from all unrighteousness. In Jesus Precious Name!

Chapter Three
Witness Protection: The Role of the Local Church

Up to this point in this book, I have been able to speak with veritable certainty as I shared facts about my life and calling with you. There is no reasonable argument against those facts that I represented because they are my historical facts. However, this is not the case for many areas concerning the Church, the Bible, and other issues relative to God or religion.

In fact, it seems to me that people love to argue about, for, and/or against spiritual issues. You can encounter the least argumentative, least opinionated person in the world ... but when the subjects of religion, or church, or Bible are broached, suddenly they are an apologist with a minor in world religions, and they are hankering for a fight. It is truly shocking at times. While I am on the subject, I also find it baffling how certain folks will sit and listen to a pastor or a teacher, time and again, only to learn what they disagree about so that on the way out of the sanctuary, they may attempt to hold a public debate concerning those "deeper truths" about which you are mistaken.

It could be comical if it wasn't so indicative of the stubbornness of the human heart, the fleshly desire to be heard, the arrogance of being right, the failure to recognize the apparent authority, and most importantly, the failure to recognize pastoral authority; all of which are an indication of a low view of the sovereignty of God. Because if you truly believed that God is sovereign, you would comprehend His control, and you would begin searching for your place within His will.

I am not suggesting that you should, or must agree with everything you hear, rather I am suggesting that we should approach each opportunity looking for and expecting agreement in the fundamental areas, and we should save the polarizing arguments for friendly discussions at the proper time, and furthermore if your pastor or your teacher offends you often, and the offense is not the convicting work of the Holy Spirit of God, you should find another place to worship and grow.

And if you have attended multiple places of worship and you just can't find a pastor, or a staff, or a teacher that you agree with, I suggest you look in the mirror of the Word of God; James 1:19-27, "Wherefore, my beloved brethren, let every man be swift to hear, slow to speak, slow to wrath: For the wrath of man worketh not the righteousness of God. Wherefore lay apart all filthiness and superfluity of naughtiness, and receive with meekness the engrafted word, which is able to save your souls. But be ye doers of the word, and not hearers only, deceiving your own selves. For if any be a hearer of the word, and not a doer, he is like unto a man beholding his natural face in a glass: For he beholdeth himself, and goeth his way, and straightway forgetteth what manner of man he was. But whoso looketh into the perfect law of liberty, and continueth therein, he being not a forgetful hearer, but a doer of the work, this man shall be blessed in his deed. If any man among you seem to be religious, and bridleth not his tongue, but deceiveth his own heart, this man's religion is vain. Pure religion and undefiled before God and the Father is this, To visit the fatherless and widows in their affliction, and to keep himself unspotted from the world." With that and in the timeless words and wisdom of the old sage Forrest Gump, "that is all I have to say about that..."

Let us move on to our original subject...

Why did I say all of that? Quite simply, there is debate about the biblical role of the local church is, or what it is supposed to be. I am sure that you are aware of the debate, even if you are not aware of the details. This debate has led to doctrinal splits, denominational divisions, and church splits, and it has led some to leave the "church" altogether. It is most assuredly not the only debate, but it is there just the same.

The purpose of this book is not to wade into those debates; it would be a wasteful use of this space. Rather, I want to present you with a real, nuts-and-bolts answer while seeking to remain biblically centered.

I suppose we should begin by determining what the church is. Is it a building? Is it a body of people? Is it a hierarchical organization? I believe most of us know the very basic answer to this question. Just a cursory search through Google or some other search engine will give you a one- or two-line answer that is sufficient for almost any conversation.

The first time we see the word "church" used in the New Testament is in the Gospel of Matthew, chapter 16 and verse 18, to be exact. This is a significant passage because in it the *Ekklesia* is first mentioned in relation to the work of Christ. That is, the called-out assembly. In response to Peter's confession of Christ as the Messiah, the Son of God, Jesus says, "Upon this Rock (this confession of truth) I will build my Church, and the gates of hell will not prevail against it." And so, we are introduced to the idea that Jesus will establish a called-out assembly, a group of people called apart, out from among the others, based upon the truth that Jesus is the Christ, the Son of the Living God.

We don't see anything else concerning the Church until the day of Pentecost. On that day the disciples of Jesus, (about 120 individuals who were the *Ekklesia*, the called-out assembly, Acts 1:12-15) having just received the gift of the Holy Spirit (Acts 2:4), and being led of the Spirit began to preach "the wonderful works of God" in every man's language (tongues) so that all who heard could understand (Acts 2:6, 8,11).

Peter, then being filled with the Holy Spirit of God and challenged by the mockers, stood to preach. Beginning at Joel, he displayed for them the truths of scripture and its fulfillment, and then he preached to them the Lord Jesus, who came in the fulfillment of scriptures, yet was delivered according to the wickedness of the hearts of men and according to the foreknowledge of God to be crucified. Whom God had raised from the dead and had made Him both Lord and Christ. *I hope you know Him!*

Verse 37 of Acts chapter 2 says, "When they heard this, they were pricked in their heart, and said unto Peter and the rest of the apostles, "Men and brethren, what shall we do?" At this time, Peter would call for their repentance and baptism. The result of this was that "They gladly received" (Acts 2:41) his word, and there were added unto them about three thousand souls. This is the beginning of the Church as we know it.

A consideration of the next several verses in Acts 2 would show some characteristics of the Church as Christ intended it. They were united in *doctrine*, in *fellowship*, in breaking of bread, in prayer, praising God, and *having favor with all people*. We could extrapolate this example and speak of the "having in common, and the house-to-house fellowship, and the daily dwelling in the temple," but we would recognize some cultural diversities. We do, however, see the bones of the New Testament Church in this passage; it is a group of people who have been saved, born again, and who are united in doctrine, fellowship, and prayer, who are daily praising God, and who are hard to speak evil of.

I would remind you that this book is not intended to be an exposition of Church doctrine. This definition, which will continue, is given to establish the functional purpose of the Church in hopes of arriving at an agreement on how you may help the local church.

With that stated, let me also remind you that we do not derive or develop our church doctrine from the book of the Acts of the Apostles. This book is a historical account of the birth and establishment of the New Testament Church, which church was an apostolic church under the dominion of the apostles. The office of apostles closed with the death of John the Beloved, and the apostolic dominion ceased.

The apostle Paul was given the revelation of the Church age in which we reside. To him was given the doctrine of the church under which we operate. If we were going to have an expositional doctrinal discussion concerning the Church, we would begin with the writings of the Apostle Paul, but we are not; we are simply establishing what the church is and what it is not. And I believe we have accomplished that. The Church is a group of people united in salvation. We could go further and reference the fact that the church is an organism rather than an organization. This organism is represented in the Bible as a Body; in fact, it is the Body of Christ, and He is the head. It is also represented as the Bride of Christ, yet again a body and organism.

Note the following scriptures: Romans 12:4-5, "For as we have many members in *one body*, and all members have not the same office: So we, being many, are *one body* in Christ, and every one members one of another."

And 1 Corinthians 10:16-17, "The cup of blessing which we bless, is it not the communion of the blood of Christ? The bread which we break, is it not the communion of the body of Christ? For _we being many are one bread, and one body_: for we are all partakers of that one bread."

And 1 Corinthians 12:12-13, "Now _ye are the body_ of Christ, and members in particular. For by one Spirit are we all baptized into _one body,_ whether we be Jews or Gentiles, whether we be bond or free; and have been all made to drink into one Spirit._"_

And 1 Corinthians 12:27, "Now _ye are the body_ of Christ, and members in particular. And also Colossians 1:18 – "And he is the head _of the body, the church:_ who is the beginning, the firstborn from the dead; that in all things he might have the preeminence."

Colossians 1:24, "Who now rejoice in my sufferings for you, and fill up that which is behind of the afflictions of Christ in my flesh for his _body's sake, which is the church._"

Colossians 2:19, "And not holding the Head, from which _all the body_ by joints and bands having nourishment ministered, and knit together, increaseth with the increase of God."

And lastly, Ephesians 4:15-16, "But speaking the truth in love, may grow up into him in all things, which is the head, even Christ: From whom _the whole body_ fitly joined together and compacted by that which every joint supplieth, according to the effectual working in the measure of every part, maketh increase of the body unto the edifying of itself in love." (*Added emphasis mine)

There are many other references, but I believe it is clear that the Church is the body of believers, all joined together, connected in doctrine, duty, diligence, and fellowship. We will discuss the body further in the next chapter as we consider biblical church membership.

So, the Church is not a building. Rather, it is a Body. Does this negate the importance of the church building? Absolutely not; the church building is a tool. It is necessary in the climate and culture in which we live. Over the years, I have had several folks inform me that they don't need to come to the church building proper to have church. And the conversation typically continues in a defensive tone concerning how they can (and do) have church in other places. It could be at the lake, in the cove, at the ball field between games, at the rodeo between events, in their car on the way to the beach, or at the beach in the early mornings with their families, as if I, the pastor, have never been to the beach with my family and attempted to have an early morning devotion, the locations for these impromptu and usually excusatory church services are almost as limitless as the proverbial liver pills of Mr. Carter. Again, we will consider this subject more deeply in the following chapter; suffice it to say that the church building, while not the Church, is an important aspect of the Church's biblical role in the community as it provides a base of operations from which the Church, the literal body of believers, can launch in order to fulfill their calling.

Hopefully, we agree that the Church is a body rather than a building. Next, we must ask and answer the question: Is the Church a hierarchical organization?

Let's begin with a helpful definition. What is a hierarchical organization? The following definition is available at Wikipedia and will be sufficient for this discussion. "A hierarchical organization is an organizational structure where every entity in the organization, except one, is subordinate to a single other entity. This arrangement is a form of a hierarchy. In an organization, the hierarchy usually consists of a singular/group of power at the top with subsequent levels of power beneath them. This is the dominant mode of organization among large organizations; most corporations, governments, criminal enterprises, and organized religions are hierarchical organizations with different levels of management, power or authority. For example, the broad, top-level overview of the general organization of the Catholic Church consists of the Pope, then the Cardinals, then the Archbishops, and so on." Another organization defined hierarchy as a pyramid, where all answer to the top of the pyramid.

For the purposes of our discussion, we are considering the "United" denominations, such as the Catholic Church, the United Methodist Church, the PCA, or the USPCA, the Episcopalian Church, the Anglican Church, etc. I am sure there are many that I am not mentioning; however, this is not supposed to be an exhaustive list. These churches are all similar in their governance, and they become the Church for their parishioners.

Even some of the larger non-denominational movements are considered hierarchical. The name non-denominational is a misnomer because once they identify themselves as non-denominational, they have identified themselves with an entire movement, which is the literal definition of denomination. Consider the trusty Wikipedia once again, "A religious denomination is a subgroup within a religion that operates under a common name, tradition, and identity." This identification with others is not, however, what makes them hierarchical; the governing boards that oversee them do that. For example, one very common non-denominational mega-church in the Southeast is literally an arm of the Wesleyan Church International. Also, we must consider almost any church that has multiple campuses, with one senior pastor overall, as a form of hierarchy at least, and many times, they are operating under the auspices of Apostolic authority. The autonomy of the local church is what separates the Baptists, and even the Southern Baptists from this group.

Now, back to our original question: Is the Church a hierarchical organization? The answer is no. There may be a portion of the true church, the Body of Christ, housed inside the hierarchical churches of the world, but the hierarchical church is an organization and not an organism.

So, we are back to the singular conclusion. The true Church is the Body of believers. It is not the building, though the building is important. It is not the hierarchical organization, which is unnecessary; it is the congregation of born-again believers.

It is the living organism that consists of every born-again believer since Pentecost. More apropos for the conversation at hand, the church is composed of all born-again believers who are living today. As a means of further clarification, we would also add that the local church is composed of all born-again believers who meet in a particular facility.

Now that we know what the Church is, we can answer the question for which this chapter is named: What is the biblical role of the Church? We have shown that the church is a group of people united in salvation, continuing together in doctrine, fellowship, breaking of bread, and prayers. We have also shown that they will be continually praising the Lord and will be hard to speak against. But all of this is to what end? For what purpose?

I believe we should consider The Great Commission at this moment. We see the complete version of that in Matthew 28:19-20, but there are aspects of it in Mark 16:15, Luke 24:14, and even John 20:21. And then in Acts 1:8, we see another clear representation of the commission. In each case, the preaching of the Word of God, the teaching of the Word of God, and the baptizing of the converts are prominent. In Acts 1:8, we are informed that the power for this task will come from the indwelling Holy Spirit of God, and we are told to be witnesses unto the person, power, and preeminence of Jesus.

As we read the New Testament, we understand that the Christian is supposed to "Love God with all your heart, soul, and mind" and "Love your neighbor as yourself." We are to keep the commandments of the Lord. Later, we are told that the Church should also provide for the fatherless and the widows. We are to pray without ceasing. We are to always be abounding in the work of the Lord. There are many responsibilities mentioned.

Are these responsibilities separate from the Church or in conjunction with it? And what about the immediate culture that we live in? Do they impact these responsibilities? Food pantries and clothes closets, homeless shelters, drug recovery programs, women's ministry, men's ministry, children's ministry, youth ministry, special needs ministry, recreational leagues, etc....

Are these ministries right? Are they wrong? Are they marginal? Are they misplaced? Are they necessary? We will close this chapter by looking at Acts 1:8 again.

Acts 1:8, "But ye shall receive power, after that the Holy Ghost is come upon you: and *ye shall be witnesses unto me* both in Jerusalem, and in all Judea, and in Samaria, and unto the uttermost part of the earth." (*Added emphasis mine.)

This is the root Biblical role of the Church and of the Christian in the world today. We are to be witnesses unto Jesus, His person, power, and preeminence. These other ministries are just a means to an end. They are not bad, but they are only good as they point others to Him.

How do you suppose our churches are doing today? How many of the events, outreaches, fellowships, and ministries exist for reasons other than "witnessing unto Him?" Would you pray with me?

God give us eyes to see. Ears to hear. A desire to obey. And the courage to follow you wholly. Lord, we need a Revival in our land, Lord we need a stirring in our land, Lord we need an awakening in our land. Father shake us from the doldrums of mediocrity and give us a vision of the grandeur and glory of our Immutable, Eternal, Omniscient, Omnipotent, and Omnipresent Creator, Sustainer, and Savior! Lord help us to witness unto Him! It's in the precious name of our Savior the Lord Jesus Christ that we pray! Amen.

Chapter Four
The One Person Your Church Can't Do Without

Here we find ourselves with yet another question, the answer of which could be subjective. Possibly even controversial. The question is, what does biblical church membership look like? If we remove the qualifier "biblical" the answer is most definitely subjective because it is then defined by denomination, or personal bent, or even worse the by-laws of a particular church.

However, when we use the qualifier "biblical," it at least ties us to the Bible. We may still need to worry about some subjectivity, and we may struggle with various differing views, cultural arguments, or doctrinal disagreements, but nonetheless, we are grounded in one body of work.

We cannot read any details about church membership in the Gospels because there was not yet a church to be a member of prior to Pentecost. We may indeed learn various applicable truths in a proper study of the gospels that would speak to attitude, service, worship, prayer, and many other Christian living principles, but these would only be relative to church membership as they are relative to the Christian.

We are introduced to the first one hundred and twenty church members in Acts chapter 1. They are the founders, if you will *(light sarcasm)*. We notice immediately that they are all in one accord, that is, in agreement, in attitude, or in opinion. Secondly, we notice that they are gathered in a particular place; next, we note that they are waiting on a visitation from the Lord; and lastly, we see that they are praying. There is some profundity in this scene; therefore, in some sense, we would do well to imitate them.

Other than these simple observations, we do not know much about them, and we are not given much insight as to their relationship with one another. Before we can discover much about them, they are filled with the Holy Spirit of God, and we are off to the races.

There is a spiritual outbreak, a demonstration of power, a sermon that convicts (still not a bad description for a biblical church service), and suddenly, there are 3,120 of them.

Once we add these 3,000, we get another description; we discussed it in the previous chapter. Those who were saved were baptized, and then they continued steadfastly (faithfully) in doctrine, fellowship, breaking of bread, prayer, praising the Lord, and blessing the community. And as many as would be saved were added to the Church. They were added daily.

Concerning this group, we are informed that they sold all their possessions, had all things in common, were in the temple daily, and went from house to house, breaking bread with singleness of heart. Before long, thousands more were counted. There were persecutions, threats, displays of power, and martyrdom.

If this were all we had for a definition of biblical church membership, I dare say attendance would likely plummet. We can see some similarities, but there are obvious cultural differences and spiritual differences as well because this is part of the Apostolic movement.

So, while we can take simple outlines of how they met, agreed, shared fellowship, and prayed together, we can obviously see that they belonged to a separate era, and application then becomes difficult.

As we move into the Pauline works, we began to catch glimpses of New Testament Church membership. There are still cultural and generational diversities, but we can begin to see what communion and fellowship really look like, we can see how to make application of having all things in common, we can comprehend being in the temple daily, and we understand what it means to be in one accord. We see these things and begin to understand them because Paul, under the inspiration of the Holy Spirit of God begins to explain how we are all one body. We are immersed (baptized) into the body of Christ, and now we are many members but one body.

So, our communion, our fellowship, is in the body of Christ. We have all things in common because we are one body. Physically, we live apart from one another, we work apart from one another, and we play apart from one another, but spiritually, we are united in the Body of Christ.

We learn that our body is the temple of the Holy Spirit of God. It is our tabernacle, but it is His temple, and we dwell in the temple every day. You in your body, and me in my body, but we in the Body of Christ. And just as there is only one body, there is also only one Spirit. The same Spirit that indwells me, also indwells you. We have that in common; we have that connection to Him and to one another. So that when we come into contact, the spirit in me testifies with the spirit in you, and we both know that we are children of God.

The Apostle Paul uses the metaphor of the human body in several passages, in Romans, Corinthians, Ephesians, and Colossians. He carries that metaphor to spectacular exhibit in 1 Corinthians 12:12-27.

Let's take a moment to consider this passage as we consider biblical church membership. I think it is easier than we make it out to be, while at the same time being harder than advertised.

Note first; 1 Corinthians 12:12-27, "For as the body is one, and hath many members, and all the members of that one body, being many, are one body: so also is Christ. For by one Spirit are we all baptized into one body, whether we be Jews or Gentiles, whether we be bond or free; and have been all made to drink into one Spirit. For the body is not one member, but many."

Here, in these verses, the penman makes it clear that the Church is one body and that the one body is Christ. There are many of us, but when we are born again, and the Holy Spirit takes up residence in us, we are then immersed (baptized) into the Body with all the other born-again, spirit-filled believers. Our nationality doesn't matter, our privilege or lack thereof doesn't matter, our background doesn't matter. The only thing that matters is that we are filled with the Spirit of God, which is the case for every born-again believer. So, the initial entry into the Church is worry-free stress-free; it is not a chore or a work; it is a grace benefit provided by the Spirit of God. If you are born again, you are a member of the body.

Note next; 1 Corinthians 12:15-16, "If the foot shall say, Because I am not the hand, I am not of the body; is it therefore not of the body? And if the ear shall say, Because I am not the eye, I am not of the body; is it therefore not of the body?"

In verses 15-16 we begin to see some of the human element of this membership. What if I become self-conscious about my given position in the body? What if I decide that I am unhappy with my membership? What if I decide that I don't care for my position? Or I decide that I no longer want to participate? Can I just refuse, can I just withdraw, can I just determine that I am no longer a part of the body?

It looks like the answer to that is "No." Paul says that even if a member determines to no longer be a part of the body, it is still attached to the body. When you consider this in the physical sense, your hand has no authority over itself, and your eye has no authority over itself, and so on. There is some connection herein to the eternal security of the believer. This may not be the most likely passage from which to present that truth, but obviously, we can see that we do not maintain our own place in the body as much as we receive it, likewise our Salvation is not something that we have obtained, or acquired through struggle and pay rather it is a gift that has been given, a birth that has taken place, and once you've been born it is impossible to be unborn.

Also notice; 1 Corinthians 12:17-20, "If the whole body were an eye, where were the hearing? If the whole were hearing, where were the smelling? But now hath God set the members every one of them in the body, as it hath pleased him. And if they were all one member, where were the body? But now are they many members, yet but one body."

We also notice that each member has a specific purpose. They are mostly diverse from one another, and they are there to make the body complete and functional. There are many members but one body.

So, we can see the importance of member participation. Just as we would not be physically whole if one of our members stopped working, then neither is the church whole unless all its members are functioning as they are designed to function.

1 Corinthians 12:21, "And the eye cannot say unto the hand, I have no need of thee: nor again the head to the feet, I have no need of you."

Again, we notice that the members have no real authority over one another. The head cannot arbitrarily decide that it doesn't need the feet, or the eye cannot discard the hand.

Thus, it is within the Body of Christ. We can cause division, but we should not. Because God has placed each member where they are needed. And as the Apostle continues, he states that some members might seem to be feeble or dispensable, but they are not; they only have a diverse function.

1 Corinthians 12:22-24, "Nay, much more those members of the body, which seem to be more feeble, are necessary: And those members of the body, which we think to be less honorable, upon these we bestow more abundant honor; and our uncomely parts have more abundant comeliness. For our comely parts have no need: but God hath tempered the body together, having given more abundant honor to that part which lacked."

Furthermore, there should be no division, debate, or argument among the members of the body; all should care for one another.

Just imagine if your physical body began to attack itself, and it began to devour another part of itself. That is a sickness, a disease, a cancer, and we do all that we can to eradicate it in the physical body. This is what Paul is speaking of in 1 Corinthians 12:25, "That there should be no schism in the body; but that the members should have the same care one for another." Just as our physical body is well together, or sick together, every member affects the others, so it is with the Church, the Body of Christ as noted in 1 Corinthians 12:26, "And whether one member suffer, all the members suffer with it; or one member be honored, all the members rejoice with it. Now ye are the body of Christ, and members in particular."

This is church membership at the spiritual level, the true church, the eternal church. We (the born-again believers) are in it by the grace of God, and we will remain in it by the grace of God. We didn't earn a membership, and we are not responsible for maintaining it. Again, this is at the spiritual level. The metaphor breaks down a bit in the physical sense. Because in the Church some members do exhibit control over others. Sometimes a stronger member will overrule a weaker member. Sometimes a member will assume authority or position for which they are not gifted.

So, one aspect of biblical church membership is knowing your gifting and calling and being faithful to both.

But what about actual, physical church membership? What does the Bible say about that? The apostle Paul also shares some truths on this in the book of Ephesians.

Ephesians 4:11-16, "And he gave some, apostles; and some, prophets; and some, evangelists; and some, pastors and teachers; For the perfecting of the saints, for the work of the ministry, for the edifying of the body of Christ: Till we all come in the unity of the faith, and of the knowledge of the Son of God, unto a perfect man, unto the measure of the stature of the fullness of Christ: That we henceforth be no more children, tossed to and fro, and carried about with every wind of doctrine, by the sleight of men, and cunning craftiness, whereby they lie in wait to deceive; But speaking the truth in love, may grow up into him in all things, which is the head, even Christ: From whom the whole body fitly joined together and compacted by that which every joint supplieth, according to the effectual working in the measure of every part, maketh increase of the body unto the edifying of itself in love."

This passage speaks to the physical and/or literal aspects of church membership. It also speaks to various gifts and abilities and their purpose. Of course, this is not an exhaustive list of gifts and abilities, but from this list, we can see that gifts are given to individuals in view of their service to the Body of Christ and, indeed, to the development of the local assembly of believers.

There are a few key phrases that I believe we should pay attention to as we consider the question of biblical church membership. Notice first in verse 12, "For the perfecting of the saints, for the work of the ministry," we see the word "perfecting," and we know that this is speaking of completion or maturity; it is speaking of the thorough or complete equipping of the believers. What are the believers being equipped for? For the work of the ministry. And there is no mystery in the word "ministry." We see that in Greek, it is simply the word *diakonia*, and we all recognize this word; it is the same word used in Acts chapter 6 to describe the need for help in the daily distribution. We use the transliterated word "deacon" to describe these men today but in the truest sense of the word, it simply means servant. So, these gifts were given to grow, mature, and complete the saints as servants to the ministry. But wait, there's more.

Look at the remainder of verse 12, "for the edifying of the body of Christ," that is, the building up, the constructing of the body of Christ, literally the development of the Church. In God's plan, when a person receives Christ as their Savior, they are filled with the Holy Spirit of God, baptized, immersed into the body of Christ, which is the Church, and once in the church, they are gifted with particular gifts and abilities, and then consecrated to a particular service, for the strengthening, and development of the Body. This happens at the universal, or the true church level, that is, the Church, which is composed of all the born-again believers since Pentecost. But even more importantly, it happens at the immediate and local level of the Church as well. Every born-again believer is a member of the

Universal Church, but each should be an active, participative member of a local Body of believers as well.

We may wonder: How long? How long do we need to participate in the Body of Christ? Well, the penman states that we are to do so until we arrive at the following stage, "Till we all come in the unity of the faith, and of the knowledge of the Son of God, unto a perfect man, unto the measure of the stature of the fullness of Christ," that is until we experience complete unity. Until we are perfect, whole, lacking nothing, and until we measure up to the measure of the stature of Christ. I am relatively sure that no one will experience this level of perfection until we see Him and stand in His presence. 1 John 3:2, "Beloved, now are we the sons of God, and it doth not yet appear what we shall be: but we know that, when he shall appear, we shall be like him; for we shall see him as he is."

Lastly, we see the outcome of proper church membership, "**16**From whom the whole body fitly joined together and compacted by that which every joint supplieth, according to the effectual working in the measure of every part, maketh increase of the body unto the edifying of itself in love," when we all work together, as God intends, we see the Church comes together as an organism and is built up in love.

We started this chapter by asking, "What is biblical church membership?" I believe we have answered this question in a couple of ways.

First, the born-again believer is baptized by the Holy Spirit of God into the Body of Christ (aka the Universal Church), and spiritually, this is eternal; once we are in the body, we will remain there.

Then, physically, we are to be joined to a Body of believers as directed by the Lord, wherein we can exercise our spiritual gifts and abilities for the maturing of the saints, in the work of the ministry, and for the building up of the Body. We are to do this actively and participate until we are face-to-face with Christ.

Are you involved in a local assembly of believers? Are you exercising your spiritual gifts and abilities to the benefit of other believers? Are you doing the work of the ministry, are you serving in a local church?

Would you pray with me now and ask the Lord to help you find a church home or become active in your current church home? It will require commitment, but if you are a born-again believer, it is your calling, and the church needs you.

Heavenly Father, thank you for saving my soul, thank you for adding me to the church, thank you for the gifts and abilities that you have given me, and Lord, thank you for my place in the body of Christ! I am repenting now of my failure to be involved, to exercise my gifts, and to be faithful to the ministry. Lord, please forgive me and help me to find my place. Give me a burden for the church, for my community, and for a commitment to serve.

Chapter Five
Renters and Consumers: Typical Modern Members

The first two chapters were obviously testimonial, chapters 3-4 were biblically centered, and the next two chapters will be experiential.

In chapters 5 and 6, I will share my experience with church membership over the past 22 years. Some of this experience was as a church member interacting with other members, some as a deacon attempting to minister to other members, some as a minister of education attempting to recruit other members, some as an assistant pastor attempting to motivate other members, and some as a senior pastor attempting to lead other members.

I have divided my thoughts concerning church membership into two chapters: typical (or common) membership and atypical (uncommon) membership. Let's begin by considering what typical church membership looks like in the 21st century.

When I first began to outline this book, I titled this chapter "Hey Kids, We Have a New Hobby." Because, in my experience, that is how many folks treat church membership. It is a hobby, but not just a hobby. Rather, it is yet another hobby among the many that they (as a family) already participate in. So, when they find the perfect church to become members of, they insert it in their calendar along with dance class, gymnastics, volleyball, basketball, football, baseball, soccer, fastpitch, track, drama club, marching band, camping season, the scouts, fishing season, boating season, hunting seasons, golf, etc. Of course, all these hobbies take a back seat to careers and school, and there is the out-of-town family that we must go and see periodically, and we can't forget our involvement with the various social clubs and organizations (*these things are so important to us*).

I realize that I have likely just offended some of you. I can assure you that this is not my intention. However, if we are going to talk about typical church membership, and if we want to be honest with one another, then we must address the elephant in the room.

As a rule, the church gets what is left over from the weekly schedule of a typical family. And the activities that I just listed are legitimate in today's culture. My children are 24 and 28 respectively; they were both athletes, and they were both heavily involved in their schools. Both had lots of friends, and both participated in two or more sports each year, beginning at five years old and continuing through High School. My wife and I both worked; we were usually involved at church simultaneously with our careers, and for a time, I was in school as well. We were, to say the least, a busy family. But when I look at most families today, I have no idea how they keep up with their schedules.

In my pastoral heart, I truly believe that people desire to be involved in the church and its ministries, but their schedules are so packed and frantic that I am afraid they just don't know how.

The effect that this has had on the church at large is devastating. In many communities, churches that once were thriving have witnessed a decline in available workers and even in attending worshipers. Sundays and Wednesdays were once considered church days and therefore they were reserved from work, and practice, and competitions etc. But in the current 24-7 world that we live in, everything is fair game.

This has prompted a church movement that is less than healthy and also doctrinally compromised, wherein mega-churches have employed a multi-campus approach; they are offering services on non-traditional church days, Fridays, and Saturdays, and multiple services on Sundays, all in the name of convenience and availability. And they are well attended, so from a return of investment perspective, I can't blame them. To many, it likely seems as if the Lord is blessing this movement, but we can simply look at the current spiritual status of our communities and know that He is not.

Many families who would otherwise attend a more traditional church (pastor-led, volunteer-staffed, family-centered) will utilize these facilities for convenience. When they arrive, they are catered to, they are not needed for involvement, and much of the facility is staffed with paid employees. These families can come in for a professional-quality worship experience, followed by a generally encouraging message, while their children are entertained and/or taught by a staff of youth and children's workers, and all of this with no strings attached.

This movement has created a Walmart-type effect on many of the traditional community-oriented churches simply because they cannot compete with the schedule of offerings from these mega-churches. So, we end up with fewer churches in our communities and less personal involvement from our families. This, in turn, becomes cyclical because the church needs more volunteers, it must offer fewer programs, and the quality of the programs begins to suffer, prompting other families to leave. And visitors come but determine that the church is too small, and they choose not to return.

You may think this sounds like spilled milk or the angst of a small church pastor, but it is more than that; it is a call to action.

Typical church membership has been reduced to a name on the roll, a number among the giving units, a Pastor in time of need, and another event on the family calendar, which is already too full.

The last thing we need in 21st Century America is fewer churches. We need more churches, diverse churches (not in doctrine but in personality), and diverse pastors and preachers. We need churches that are nimble and able to serve the communities. A community is better served with five churches consisting of one to three hundred members than it is with one church consisting of one thousand members. And for clarity, I am not necessarily advocating for smaller churches. Rather, I am suggesting that more volunteer-served family churches can offer a more significant ministry.

I can hear you saying, "I thought this thing was about membership?" Well, it is. Churches do not cease being because of a lack of pastors. They don't cease to be because of facility issues. They cease to be because of a lack of sincere membership. In communities all around, there are dying churches, that are unable to grow a working membership, and it is usually not for a lack of people in the community, rather it is a lack of people who are available for "the perfecting of the saints, for the work of the ministry, for the edifying of the body of Christ: Till we all come in the unity of the faith, and of the knowledge of the Son of God, unto a perfect man, unto the measure of the stature of the fullness of Christ."

We need people who will step up and serve, who will make a commitment to grow in Grace and in the knowledge of our Lord and Savior Jesus Christ. We need sincere people who will involve their families in the life of the church and likewise involve the church in the life of their families.

People who will do more than put their name on the roll, but rather will put their heart into the ministry of the local church and seek to be witnesses unto Christ, to be working, functioning members of the body of Christ.

I mentioned that I would speak experientially, and I have done but rather vaguely. For the next page or two, I would like to share some relational experiences that I have had concerning church membership and function. My goal is not to embarrass anyone, and I certainly will not be using any names, but I will try to stay as true to the situation as possible.

Experience 1

I believe one of the more difficult experiences that I have had in the ministry has to do with funerals, and there have been several. For a while in my ministry, I was on the call list of a local funeral home who would call anytime they had an indigent family or a family who were not connected to a church. This occurred quite often, and I am a timely speaker, especially when it comes to funerals, so I was called very often. I performed funerals for all types; some were very elderly and had just lost touch with their church, some were un-churched and so they just didn't have a church family, others were from out of town and had not connected with a church family, but all of them had the commonality of having no pastor.

It was always sad as they tried to catch me up on their loved one so that the funeral would not seem impersonal. I buried folks who had church history, and I buried some who did not. I buried an infant whose family was Catholic but not observing. I buried several veterans who had little to no family and no church family, but they would receive a military service. It always broke my heart because I didn't know their spiritual destiny. However, the saddest funerals (and there were several) were for folks that were faithfully attending and contributing to a mega-church or a satellite campus, and there was no personal pastoral relationship; I would always wonder if they would be missed; and if anyone even knew that they had passed? If we are not diligent in becoming more than typical church members, if we do not rise up and recover the local church, this story will become more and more common.

Experience 2

I am currently serving as the Senior Pastor of Hoschton Baptist Church. We are an 11-year-old church plant and we have enjoyed tremendous blessings from God during those years. In the beginning, there were only 25-30 regular attending members. As we started to grow, we were acutely aware of the need for young families and programs for them. We added a few within the first 18 months, but time and time again, the response that we received from the visiting younger families was discouraging. They would say, "We love your church. The message was great, the music is just what we are looking for, and the people are very friendly, but we noticed there aren't many young families." At this point, we would share our short history, cast a vision of where we would like to go, and how we planned on arriving there. And then I would ask them to come along with us, come and help us grow, come and be the catalyst! I even began saying we need pioneers; we need young families to help us reach the other young families of our community. Yet, time and again, they would depart and go to an established church with established programs. Today we have 250 plus members. We own a facility. We are nearly debt-free.

We have active plans for additional facilities. And the one demographic that we still struggle with is the young family. I am still looking for pioneers, I am still searching for someone who will be the catalyst for other young families.

Why is that? We still get similar responses from our visitors. And I can only believe that their schedules are just too packed to become an integral part of active work. They are looking for a church that can serve their needs, that can adapt to their calendar, that can accommodate their overwrought calendar.

If we are more than the typical church member, church attendance cannot become merely an addition to our calendar. Rather, it must become the center of our lives, the orienting event of our calendar, that which all other events revolve around.

Would you pray with me right now?

Heavenly Father, I come now repenting of my busyness. Lord, I ask that you help me arrange my calendar around the body of Christ. Lord, help me become an integral part of the local church and help me, Father, be the catalyst for growth that is so desperately needed!

Chapter Six
Owners and Producers: Uncommon Members

We close the previous chapter on typical church membership with a statement similar to this; Church attendance cannot become merely an addition to your life. It needs to become the centering event of your life, that which all other events revolve around.

We have already mentioned the family calendar several times in this book. The reason for this is that there are only so many hours in a day; it is a foregone conclusion that a portion of those hours is predetermined for work and school. This is absolute; people must earn a living, and children must receive an education, and each of these events is basically non-negotiable.

What we do with the remaining hours is fully negotiable. Extracurricular activities for the children are all schedule-based. By that, I mean that you can't wait until a nondescript Saturday in May and decide that you will let your child play a team sport that day, and then on a whim (or even with research) drive to a recreational area, present your child to a team that is gathered there, and expect that they will be allowed. This entire scenario is frivolous.

Instead, you make plans to play; you purchase personal equipment, you sign up for a team, and you receive a suggested schedule for practices and a concrete schedule for games. You know the coaches and the other families involved. You may even volunteer to help coach, and then, as a family, you make a commitment for the next several weeks. You write it on your calendar; you hang the schedule on the refrigerator, and you make sure all parties are informed. And for the next 8-12 weeks everyone in the family, the workplace, and the neighborhood knows your schedule.

This scenario is true for almost every event or program you or your children will ever be involved in. And, by and large, we do not question the methods because they are the status quo. It's the same for the men's softball league, the ladies' bowling league, the fishing tournaments, and hunting seasons. We know the schedule, we record the important dates on our calendars, we let others know that we will be busy on certain dates. In the South, where we live, this scenario even applies to college football teams and their schedules.

I stress this because it sets the standard. If something is important to us, we work other aspects of life around it. We do so intentionally by making a plan, publishing the plan, and observing the plan. We do so religiously and perennially.

I know folks who have not missed a Georgia/Florida game in twenty years; that takes dedication and planning. I know men who haven't missed the opening day of deer season in fifteen years; that takes dedication, awareness, and planning. I have known families who intentionally kept their children on the same team, in the same league, with the same group of boys, and under the same coaches from t-ball to middle school in order to build chemistry and help the "program." This requires devotion to a cause and belief in a system.

I don't say any of these things in condemnation, condescension, or confrontation, as I have also done some of these things. I am simply stating that when something is important to us, we make plans, and we execute those plans. This is what is required for church membership to be uncommon or atypical. It must take precedence on your calendar and in your schedule.

Over the years, I have had church members describe to me the events that prevented them from being in a particular service; the story is usually along these lines.

"Pastor, we really enjoyed the service Sunday morning, the message was great! I was telling Tom that I wish his family could have heard it... they really need the Lord. We really wanted to be back for the service on Sunday night, this current series has been so good! I wish the rest of the church would get excited about what you are teaching, I believe it could really help them. Well, anyway, the reason we were not back was that some of our family came by after lunch, and they just stayed and stayed... we didn't think they would ever leave, but by the time they left we realized we had missed church... I really hate it happened that way, but they're family; what can you do?"

There are many things that could be said here, but the bottom line is this: the church is optional in the schedule. People go to church, as long as nothing interferes. We have every intention to be there unless someone comes over, unless something comes up, unless we have a better option. If we will be more than a typical, common church member, we will be so dedicated to attend, and to serve that our name will be synonymous with dependability. And if we do not attend the church will know immediately that something is wrong at our house.

If we make this dedication a part of who we are, our families will know. I can't imagine anyone coming to my house on a Sunday; if they know me, they know where I am going to be.

We could imagine that same situation in the context of one of the other events on your calendar, and we know that it would end much differently.

If you had a game to attend and your family came by for a visit, you would inform them posthaste. When it was time to leave, you would walk them out the door, load up your immediate bunch, and head to the venue. The adage that has been around for years (as long as I can remember) is that if you waited until Monday morning to determine whether you would go to work or not, you wouldn't have a job for long.

After our initial commitment, as a couple, to church attendance, I never remember discussing it again. We wanted to be in the Lord's house. We wanted to be with our church family. We wanted to see what the Lord would do next. We wanted to see if the people we had invited would be there. We certainly didn't want them (the people we invited) to show up and find us not there. We had jobs to do, and people were counting on us, so we did not miss, and because of that the Lord blessed us daily.

Some might object and say that their children will not participate, or that their children will resist, or that they want to give their children the freedom to choose. I want to immediately reply in honesty and transparency; this is an excuse. This isn't a parenting book, but I am willing to give some free advice, and I am also more than willing to challenge falsehood. Anything that mom and dad are committed to, and certain of, and consistent in, the children will learn it, and eventually (sooner rather than later) they will acquiesce to it.

As for the fallacy of allowing children to choose for themselves, this argument or suggestion is usually only relative to religious conversations. Typically speaking, children are not allowed to choose their schooling regimen, they are not allowed to choose their own doctors, they are not allowed to choose their own medications. In fact, just about their entire life is planned for them (and rightfully so). Why would church attendance with mom and dad be any different?

So, here we are. We are talking about uncommon, atypical church membership. Step one in church membership is exemplified by church attendance. Church attendance is planned, purposeful, prevailing, and predominant. This means that if you are faithful in church attendance, then it will be planned; it is unlikely that you will be a faithful church member/attender just simply waiting for an unimpeded opportunity to attend. Secondly, if it is legitimately planned you must be purposeful about putting it on the schedule, on the calendar, into the weekly activities for the family. If you will be purposeful then church attendance must become of prevailing and predominant importance to the family. This means that it takes a place on the calendar wherein it cannot be preempted by another event. Just as you *must* go to work, and the children *must* go to school, we all *must* go to church – with the same dedication, the same devotion, the same consideration as the other *must* on your schedule.

This will require setting aside days. Sunday and Wednesday evenings belong to the Lord. There is no question of preeminence on those days, and there is no question as to where we will be—we will be at the church.

I recently read a comment from Kevin DeYoung, which stated, "The man who attempts Christianity without the church shoots himself in the foot, shoots his children in the leg, and shoots his grandchildren in the heart."

This comment is so appropriate for this subject. Christianity is not accommodating to the family/man who does not attend Church. We need the corporate gathering; we need the familial connection, we need the community of believers, and we need the camaraderie of others who are struggling in like manner. In this environment, we realize that we are not alone, we recognize the need for the Church, and we recharge for the week of trials that lies ahead.

I have folks argue with me about the necessity of traditional, meaningful church membership. I hear the plans for "home church" and for "family church," and you may be one of the proponents for such, but if you are honest, you know that this is the minority, and many Christians need the accountability of the local assembly. They need the reassurance of the local assembly. They need the inclusion of the local assembly. I have met several families over the past 22 years who ventured down the "home church" or "family church" trail. Most of them had significant regrets, many had fallen away, many had witnessed a negative impact on their children's spiritual formation, and a few had even experienced marital difficulties due to the isolation from other like-minded couples. I find it ironic that often, someone cannot find the time or the heart to be involved at the local church level, but suddenly, they believe that they can successfully and consistently plan a worshipful, devotional teaching experience for their family.

I am certain that uncommon church membership begins with attendance—planned, purposeful, prevailing, and predominant church attendance.

Step two is involvement. Consistent, considerate, cooperative, and courageous involvement. Everything gets better with involvement. First, the involvement is an investment, and the project then takes on a personal value. Second, the involvement shows interest which leads to importance. And third the involvement breeds inclusivity, which adds diversity of experience, expectation, and expertise. The imagination is limitless when we consider the opportunities that are available for the church if all walks of people, with all walks of abilities, become committed and involved.

A church full of involved members would need little infrastructure, advertising, production, financing, maintenance, legal, IT, security, orchestration, teaching, education, or organization; the opportunities are only limited by the imagination. A church could quickly become the heartbeat of a community, a refuge, a place where every member expressed their gifts and abilities, and God would be glorified in the functionality of the Body.

But often, people are unwilling to do the very thing God gifted them in, and I comprehend this because we often exercise our gifts to earn a living, and the redundancy of doing it at work and at church can become quite tedious. But I would remind you that God has gifted you for the Body's sake.

My first service opportunity in the church was to act as the president of the adult Sunday school class.

I was asked to do this because they appreciated my organizational ability (*which some would call OCD tendencies*). My first staff position in a church was as the Minister of Education. It was also an organizational, managerial position; I was recruited for that position based on my small business and management experience. These things were the most obvious of my giftings, and I was thrilled to see that they would carry over into the church! I also discovered that the exercise of these gifts and abilities in the church environment allowed for spiritual growth in the gifting and made me a more effective manager in the workplace. (*This obviously has its limits, but the effects are real just the same*).

Please allow me one other example of God using your giftings for the good of the Body of Christ. As I have stated in my testimony, I am a mechanic by trade. I have held several other positions relative to the automotive field, but indeed, I am a mechanic, and for the most part, I enjoyed that facet of my career. After being vocationally involved in the ministry for six years or so, in my second vocational role I had the occasion to go to Lima, Peru with a group of workers. It was my second trip to Lima, and I had been on several other mission trips to Haiti. On these trips, I led groups, I preached, I served in evangelistic ways, and we completed construction projects. On this trip, the missionary discovered that I was a mechanic; he was ecstatic, but I was not… The children's home that he was overseeing owned a small import vehicle that had been donated to them as a staff car, but according to the missionary, it would not run. He asked if I would look at it. It was summer in Peru; it was hot – almost jungle hot – I didn't have work clothes, and I didn't have tools; in fact, all I had was excuses.

So, I declined for the above reasons, but after seeing his disappointment and hearing his offer to use his tools (tools ha-ha!), in just a moment or two, I repented and decided to look at it for him.

I will spare you the weepy details, but it wasn't a running problem; it was a starting problem. I diagnosed the issue and, by God's grace, removed the starter and replaced it with a new one. He was thrilled, I was nasty, the car was fixed, and guess what? God was glorified. Because I was able to exercise a gift that was given to a rebellious, self-willed boy who, by the grace of God, had been gloriously saved and later called into the ministry. Your Involvement in the Church is paramount. And it is the second step towards becoming an uncommon member.

The third step is to minister. You must attend, be involved, and minister. That is the aim of every uncommon member.

Let's say just a couple of words about how you minister. To minister is to serve. That is simply what the word means. There is always a plethora of ways to serve. There are workdays, there are special projects, there is security, IT, finance, etc. But most importantly there is the classroom, where you can affect the next generation. Think of the joy of coaching a team of boys in football and all the lessons you can impart, the joys of growth and accomplishment, and then consider that at a spiritual level. I have folks tell me all the time that they are not capable of teaching a Sunday school, Master Club, AWANA, or children's church, but this is simply not true.

You can literally do anything you set your mind and heart to and in this case, you have the blessed Holy Spirit of God to guide you. Find you a group of kids, or tweens, or teens, or young adults, or men, or women and commit to teach them and to grow with them in the grace and knowledge of the Lord Jesus Christ.

Now, before we close this chapter in prayer, allow me to introduce my thesis for this project.

For the (your) church to function (this is basic), there must be selflessness, service, and financial support (this includes you), but if the Church would flourish and catch fire (this is biblical), significant sacrifice must be added. That means that your selflessness isn't enough; you must be sacrificially selfless. Your service isn't enough; it will require your sacrificial service. And your financial support isn't enough; you must be sacrificially supportive.

We will spend the next three chapters developing this thesis and defining these sacrificial needs. At this time, would you pray with me?

Heavenly Father, would you work in our hearts to reveal to us our gifts and abilities, and then, upon that revelation, would you help us commit ourselves to faithfully attend, functionally involve, and fruitfully minister to the body of Christ? Help us, Lord, to be diligent and devoted. Amen.

Chapter Seven
The Sacrifice God Desires, and Your Church Needs

As I stated at the close of chapter 6, the thesis for this project is as follows: For the (your) church to function (this is basic), there must be selflessness, service, and financial support (this includes you), but if the Church would flourish, and catch fire; (this is biblical) significant sacrifice must be added. *That means that your selflessness isn't enough; you must be sacrificially selfless.* Your service isn't enough; it will require your sacrificial service. And your financial support isn't enough; you must be sacrificially supportive.

You will notice that I have personalized the Church parenthetically as your church. The reason for this is that unless you take ownership of the church you attend, you will never be more than a casual attendee, and casual attendance leads to casual Christianity. As the song says, "I don't want to be, I don't want to be a casual Christian, and I don't want to live, and I don't want to live a lukewarm life, because I want to light up the night with an everlasting light, I don't want to live a casual Christian life." So, it is of the utmost importance that you take ownership of your church and participate in it with intentionality.

Secondly, you will notice that I included three additional parenthetical statements. The first is in relation to the Church's functioning, which states that this is basic. The idea is not that all churches basically function, as I have known several dysfunctional churches. And given enough time, a dysfunctional church typically becomes a non-functioning church. The parenthetical statement was meant to identify the level of function. As in the basic level of being is to merely function. The point is that many churches attain the level of functioning without ever attaining the level of flourishing.

Once again, I ask you to note the need for the involvement to be personalized. This brings us to the final parenthetic statement, which is "this is biblical." Again, the thought is not that the only biblical Church is the one that is flourishing and catching fire, but rather that biblically speaking, that is the design for the New Testament Church.

The Church is intended to be victorious; it is intended to withstand the gates of Hell. The Church is seen as thriving and spreading like wildfire. It is witnessed as the "turning upside down" of society. It is declared to be the literal Body of Christ, of which Christ is the head no less. It is upsetting to see a church struggling to survive, attempting to motivate the Lord's people to serve, and constantly coming up needy. Seeing a church that struggles for finances, and facility, a church that struggles to fill the pews on a weekly basis, a church that rarely ever uses its baptismal pool. These things are saddening to the pastor; they are defeating to the servants, and they are repelling to the lost. Most of all, they are not biblical. The Church that is portrayed in the scriptures is a powerful, productive, and participative Body of believers seeking the Lord and led by the Holy Spirit.

The conclusion of the thesis is that significant sacrifice must be added to those personal involvements of service, selflessness, and financial support, so that we end up with sacrificial selflessness, sacrificial service, and sacrificial financial support. In this chapter, we will establish a definition for selflessness and sacrificial selflessness and offer some examples.

Notice first that Merriam-Webster defines selflessness as "Having no concern for self," unselfish. Dictionary.com defines it as "Lack of preoccupation with one's own interests, advancement, desires, etc., and attentiveness to those of others; unselfishness," and lastly the Cambridge Dictionary states it as, "The quality of caring more about what other people need and want than about what you yourself need and want."

Let's consider this in application to the local church.

If a church is indeed a body made up of many members, all serving one purpose, then we can immediately see how damaging self-care and/or self-awareness could be. In fact, it would be debilitating at the outset.

Consider for a moment the actual human body. When you have a toothache, that is the tooth making itself and its personal position known. Suddenly the tooth is of utmost importance. You can't think, chew, relax, speak, concentrate, or accomplish anything without worrying about the tooth. This tooth, which is merely 1 of 32 others (in a perfect scenario), should just be there along with the others doing its job, but because of some damage, infection, or overt sensitivity, it has become the focus, and this focus is robbing from the overall focus of the body.

We could literally compose this scene over and over, and the result would be the same each time. The typical, healthy person has two legs, but if one becomes disabled, it is quite noticeable in gait, ability, speed, and function. The injured leg distorts all of the other joints in the lower half of the body and the back, creating pain and discomfort until the leg is absolutely the primary focus of the entire body.

And in the extrapolation of these scenarios, the pain is isn't just while the member is injured or hurting, but the effects linger. Consider the athlete who has a severe knee injury and the mental anguish that they face in overcoming the psychological restraint that results from the injury. Sometimes, it is a fact that they never return, or they never regain the same form and impact that they once had.

If we would carry this medical thought to its limits (which I am incapable of doing), I believe we would see some other very applicable truths. For example, let's consider the amputee. This person has had a diseased limb or a catastrophic injury to a limb wherein the only medically reasonable thing to do is to remove the limb, thereby removing the disease or the damage. There is still a psychological effect that is known as phantom pain, which is defined by Wikipedia as "a perception that an individual experience relating to a limb or an organ that is not physically part of the body, either because it was removed or was never there in the first place. However, phantom limb sensations can also occur following nerve avulsion or spinal cord injury. Sensations are recorded most frequently following the amputation of an arm or a leg but may also occur following the removal of a breast, tooth, or an internal organ. Phantom limb pain is the feeling of pain in an absent limb or a portion of a limb. The pain sensation varies from individual to individual." We can see in this example that it's possible for a member to affect the body in such a way as to leave an indelible mark on the body, which continues to affect it even after the departure or removal of the member.

As we consider this in the spiritual realm we can see very clearly the negative effects of overt self-awareness, or extreme self-care. I suppose we could consider some typical ways that this reveals itself. I would warn that this consideration could be subjective, not in reality, because in reality, self-care and self-awareness that are noticeable are distracting, but it could be considered subjective as to what is noticeable or what is usual and customary self-care and/or self-awareness. As a firewall against the ideas of subjectivity, I would say this, and I would do so without any reservation: anything distracting to the Church or the overall goals of the church would qualify as "overt" self-awareness and extreme self-care. I would also like to qualify this conversation with the transparent truth, which states that we are all likely guilty of these distractions at some point in time. The objective is to limit these occurrences and correct them quickly when they are noted.

With that stated, let's consider some ways that these disturbances can reveal themselves. As a sweeping comment, I would say that anytime the personal needs or desires of the individual limit the abilities of the body to accomplish the work of the Church, we would be witnessing a form of overt self-care.

This could be as mundane as a disagreement over worship styles, qualified Bible translations, or dress styles and dress codes. When someone determines that all progress and productivity will be hindered until they are heard or until they are satisfied with the status quo, this is not only destructive but can also very quickly become iniquitous.

However, there are more insidious forms of this behavior that must be considered. Most of these are experiential for the author, but none of them are unpardonable; they only work to show the deceitfulness of the heart.

Example 1

If a person considers themselves "called" whether to preach, teach, or evangelize, they will classify themselves as a preacher or as someone called by God to share the Word. There is a certain responsibility that goes along with that calling. That calling is specifically mentioned in Ephesians Chapter 4 as a "gift given unto the Body for the perfecting of the saints and the edification of the Body." If this person refuses to participate in the ministries of the Church. Or if this person requires a certain revelation from God as to how they are to be involved, or whether they are to be involved, this becomes a distraction to and a disability to the ministry of the local Body. And it places much emphasis on that individual.

As a personal experience, I once had a gentleman who claimed the calling of God on his life, who was actively serving on staff with me (I was the minister of education) as the youth pastor. When asked to serve a once monthly rotation in the children's church, he deferred to pray and ask God and then later returned to me with the answer that he "didn't have a burden for such a ministry." Now, I realize that this may seem rather innocuous, but when we see the details (of which he and I were both very aware), we will then see the selfishness of it. The details are as follows. He was one of five young lay preachers in the church. As was I, and as was the Associate Pastor. All of us were serving in the rotation, and willingly so. It was a church revitalization project with as many needs as we had opportunities.

The bulk of the children in the children's church were staff children, and four of them were his.

It's easy to see that the need was great; he was there as the calling of God would direct. God had indeed granted him the comfort of remaining there in that ministry, and his gift and abilities would have benefited the body. But rather than receiving his responsibility and fulfilling his calling he invoked a false disclaimer.

I have witnessed this play out in many ways, even to the extent that there is no other means of fulfilling that need, and someone will still hold out to be begged or pleaded with when God has specifically gifted them to fit the need.

This can display itself with musicians, singers, song leaders, business leaders, teachers, and any position imaginable wherein an obvious gift is available to fill a need, and yet they choose not to.

So, we have the one who *refuses* to fulfill their calling.

Example 2

The person who is actively practicing their gift in the local assembly but doing so in such an individualistic way as to cause a distraction and create a disturbance. This is also debilitating. Even if they are generally effective, their attitude of individuality and resistance is noticeable. In fact, it is discouraging for those being served and disconcerting for the other leadership who may have oversight of that department of ministry.

Specifically, consider the Sunday school teacher who is capable and gifted in teaching but resists the "program" at large. For example, the program is designed to include outreach, activities, and continued training. All materials are provided, all training is provided, and the other participants in the program are striving to cooperate with the design, but this teacher, for their own personal reasons, determines to teach and lead in their own specific way contrary to the program outlined.

This is discouraging to the class as they likely feel "caught in the middle." It is disconcerting to the Sunday school director, who is valiantly attempting to fulfill his responsibilities. It is distracting to the minister of education as he seeks to guide the director through this growing pain. And it is distressing to the pastor who is seeking the overall well-being of the body but has little time for such a skirmish in the grand scheme of things.

This could also manifest in a choir member who constantly misses practice, a sound tech who constantly misses their spot in the rotation, a nursery worker who readily ignores nursery restrictions to appease their own children, or a children's church worker who determines to "do their own thing" despite an overall church plan for that department or area of ministry.

The individualist we are speaking of is resistant to overall program plans or purposes for no specific reason except that it doesn't fall within the parameters of personal preference or desire.

I have also dealt with several of these circumstances in my ministry, and I am certain others have as well. In fact, these examples are not meant to elicit any pity, or to embody any experiential expertise. Indeed, these things are all too common. I am quite confident that as you are reading this, you either have a person in mind or a circumstance wherein you were that person. The point of these examples is to point out that if we are not careful, the flesh within will rise up and more than validate any negative behavior that we express; it will use the deceitfulness of our own hearts to exonerate our own guilt.

What is the answer? The answer generically is selflessness. We must remove self from the equation as much as possible. I believe that this is akin to the conversation about spiritual maturity. Suffice it to say that some are more capable than others in this manner. Also important is the understanding that this is a developmental trait that is generally connected to the progressive sanctification of the believer.

So, there should be continual growth that occurs with our spiritual maturity.

We do not have to look far for scriptural support for selflessness. Any number of passages from within the Pauline epistles would serve as sufficient grounds for understanding in this subject. We will list a few here and likely use them several times over the next few chapters.

Keep in mind we are establishing the case for selflessness, and we will also be considering sacrificial selflessness.

Romans 12:1-16 says, "I beseech you therefore, brethren, by the mercies of God, that ye present your bodies a *living sacrifice, holy, acceptable unto God, which is your reasonable service.* And be not conformed to this world: but be ye transformed by the renewing of your mind, that ye may prove what is that good, and acceptable, and perfect, will of God. For I say, through the grace given unto me, to every man that is among you, *not to think of himself more highly than he ought to think;* but to think soberly, according as God hath dealt to every man the measure of faith. *For as we have many members in one body,* and all members have not the same office: So, we, being many, are one body in Christ, and *every one members one of another.* Having then gifts differing according to the grace that is given to us, whether prophecy, let us prophesy according to the proportion of faith; Or ministry, let us wait on our ministering: or he that teacheth, on teaching; Or he that exhorteth, on exhortation: he that giveth, let him do it with simplicity; he that ruleth, with diligence; he that sheweth mercy, with cheerfulness. *Let love be without dissimulation.* Abhor that which is evil; cleave to that which is good. Be kindly affectioned one to another with brotherly love; in honor *preferring one another;* Not slothful in business; fervent in spirit; serving the Lord; Rejoicing in hope; patient in tribulation; continuing instant in prayer;

Distributing to the necessity of saints; given to hospitality. Bless them which persecute you: bless, and curse not. Rejoice with them that do rejoice, and weep with them that weep. *Be of the same mind one toward another. Mind not high things but condescend to men of low estate. Be not wise in your own conceits."*

1 Corinthians 1:26-31 says, "For ye see your calling, brethren, how that not many wise men after the flesh, not many mighty, not many noble, are called: But God hath chosen the foolish things of the world to confound the wise; and God hath chosen the weak things of the world to confound the things which are mighty; And base things of the world, and things which are despised, hath God chosen, yea, and things which are not, to bring to nought things that are: *That no flesh should glory in his presence. But of him are ye in Christ Jesus,* who of God is made unto us wisdom, and righteousness, and sanctification, and redemption: That, according as it is written, *He that glorieth, let him glory in the Lord."*

1 Corinthians 12:12-14 says, *"For as the body is one, and hath many members, and all the members of that one body, being many, are one body:* so also, is Christ. For by one Spirit are we all baptized into one body, whether we be Jews or Gentiles, whether we be bond or free; and have been all made to drink into one Spirit. *For the body is not one member, but many."*

Galatians 2:19-20 says, *"For I through the law am dead to the law, that I might live unto God.* I am crucified with Christ: nevertheless, I live; yet not I, but Christ liveth in me: and *the life which I now live in the flesh I live by the faith of the Son of God,* who loved me, and gave himself for me."

Ephesians 4:1-6 says, "I therefore, *the prisoner of the Lord, beseech you that ye walk worthy of the vocation* wherewith ye are called, with all lowliness and meekness, with long suffering, *forbearing one another in love; Endeavoring to keep the unity of the Spirit in the bond of peace. There is one body, and one Spirit,* even as ye are called in one hope of your calling; One Lord, one faith, one baptism, One God, and Father of all, who is above all, and through all, and in you all."

Philippians 1:21 says, "For to me *to live is Christ,* and to die is gain."

Philippians 2:5-8 says, "Let *this mind be in you,* which was also in Christ Jesus: Who, being in the form of God, thought it not robbery to be equal with God: But made himself of *no reputation,* and took upon him the *form of a servant,* and was made in the likeness of men: And being found in fashion as a man, he *humbled hi*mself, and *became obedient unto death,* even the death of the cross."

Any of these Scriptures will suffice to support the idea of selflessness. That is, we are a part of something that is bigger than ourselves. We are no longer independent; we are incorporated into the Body of Christ.

I once heard a missionary speak out of Matthew 14 concerning the feeding of the 5,000. This missionary was a very strong preacher; he had a great reputation of service, and he had accomplished some terrific things in the ministry by God's grace. As he shared the details of the feeding of the 5,000, he issued the challenge that we should desire to be a part of something bigger than ourselves. Time and again, over and over throughout that sermon, he issued the challenge that the believers should desire to be a part of something bigger than themselves. At the time, I was so convicted because he was issuing the call to the ministry, which I had already answered, but I wanted to be obedient, and the Spirit was moving me to do more.

However, now, after twenty years of service and ministry experience, twenty years of continued biblical study, and more than a decade of pastoral experience, I have come to realize that we *are* a part of something bigger than ourselves – as soon as we accept Christ as our Savior! We do not need to become or seek to be; we already are part of the Body of Christ. That is much bigger than the self, but the self has a strong desire to live, and so it constantly rears its old ugly head and seeks to separate from the Body so that it may express its individualism. This we must resist. We must fight the desire to express ourselves and seek rather to express Christ, who has raised us from the dead and now resides within.

This is selflessness. Just the expression of the Body of which we are a part. I am certainly not advertising it as an easy thing to do, but it is the basic expectation of every born-again believer. We are many members, but one body, and we should express that unity in its simplest form by expressing selflessness.

However, in accordance with our thesis statement, we have stated that selflessness is required for the Church to function at the basic level, but if the Church is to flourish, which is biblical, then sacrificial selflessness will be required.

How would we define sacrificial selflessness? We have already discussed the idea of selflessness, but as a reminder, we will repeat the Cambridge dictionary definition, which states it as "the quality of caring more about what other people need and want than about what you yourself need and want." So, how would we consider this in relation to sacrificial selflessness?

Obviously, the word sacrificial means "of or relating to sacrifice." When we investigate the definition of the word sacrifice, we see several meanings that are relevant, such as the act of offering something precious or suffering the loss of, giving up, renouncing, injuring, or destroying – especially for an ideal, belief, or end. These are all found in Merriam-Webster's definition. The one that I believe is most apropos, also found in Merriam-Webster's, states it this way: "the destruction of or surrender of something for the sake of something else, or something given up or lost."

In fact, the dictionary gives the example of a "parent's sacrifice for their children." That is an interesting application. Think of the way most folks sacrifice for their children; this is typically a great example of sacrificial selflessness. The mother who stays awake all night to comfort a sick child. The father works extra hours to provide some special education or training for their child. The parents who wear decades-old clothes and rarely treat themselves to even the basest of luxuries so that they provide a better home or a safer neighborhood for their children.

Consider the spouse who becomes a 24-hour caregiver, selflessly providing care for that mate as long as necessary, or the child who becomes a caregiver for an aging parent. These are examples of sacrificial selflessness. And they happen regularly, so it's not that we are incapable. However, they are less apparent and less often expressed in the Body of Christ.

But sacrificial selflessness is often the calling, it is often the need, and it is often the difference between a church functioning and a church flourishing.

It is not as regularly occurring as basic selflessness, and it is not even as often noted as carnal selfishness, but we do see this sacrificial selflessness, and likely, we each have expressed it at some point in our Christian walk. The challenge is to express it more and more as we see the need and as we feel the conviction.

Maybe you would ask for a specific example. Well, at a minimum, I offer you the antithesis of the former examples of selfishness. The person who has the calling of God on their lives, who willingly fulfills any need that the church presents even if it is not to their fulfillment or even their personal desires, would step up much like David did in 1 Samuel 17 and simply say "Is there not a cause?"

Or to the overtly qualified yet individualistic teacher, leader, singer, and worker: why not just do as the leadership asks, trusting that God has directed them in the management of the programs and ministries? I realize that it is a sacrifice of who you are (I struggle with individualism as well) but if the Lord has gifted you to serve and not called you to lead, then why not just follow the leadership that God has in place, and glory in the name of the Lord?

Experience 3

I have been particularly blessed in my current pastorate as, on several occasions, the Lord would send in a leader on loan. In each of these cases, these individuals have come in, and there have been several, who were former pastors. In each instance I have welcomed them and expressed to them that they are welcome to safe harbor for any length of time. On nearly every occasion these men have stepped up and performed tasks that are below their qualifications, and they have done so as unto the Lord, with a most excellent spirit, and to the benefit of the church. I have had pastors who served as worship leaders, choir members, pianists, Sunday School teachers, evangelism leaders, deacons, and more. I am always blessed by these men and their sacrificial selflessness. We have had ladies come through who were pianists and musicians, and while they are with us, it is always an immense blessing.

We also experience the businessmen or tradesmen who come in and just get busy exercising the gifts that God has given them. This is always a great blessing to the ministry, and often, these men are busy. They have a hectic career, a full personal life, and may even be raising children, but they come in and see the need and fill the need, no questions asked! This is sacrificial selflessness.

I am thankful for these examples, but there is always room for the born-again believers to express their gifts and abilities in the Body of Christ. And I would remind you that if every born-again believer would find their place in the Body of Christ, the local assembly would be well provided for and lacking no skill or office.

As we close this chapter, would you pray with me?

Heavenly Father, help us find our place in the church and lose ourselves in the process. Lord help us to see the body in need, the limping, and often lame local assembly striving to fulfill the great commission. As we see it Lord, affect our hearts with the need so that we would exercise sacrificial selflessness to see that the needs are met and that the body is served. And Lord we ask sincerely that you would send laborers. The harvest is plenteous, and the laborers are few. Amen.

Chapter Eight
The Work Only You Can Do

Let's remind ourselves of the thesis for this project. For the (your) church to function (this is basic), there must be selflessness, service, and financial support (this includes you), but if the Church would flourish and catch fire (this is biblical), significant sacrifice must be added. That means that your selflessness isn't enough; you must be sacrificially selfless. *Your service isn't enough; it will require your sacrificial service.* And your financial support isn't enough; you must be sacrificially supportive.

The Apostle Paul states in Romans 12:1, "I beseech you therefore, brethren, by the mercies of God, that ye present your bodies a living sacrifice, holy, acceptable unto God, which is your reasonable service." We will spend the majority of our focus in this chapter on the phrase *"which is your reasonable service."*

In Chapter 2, I stated that I am always surprised or at least intrigued that we (believers) are not more in tune with the expectations of the new birth, specifically as it relates to the price that was paid, the manner in which it was paid, and the reasonable expectations of such a sacrifice. As I stated in that chapter, we are raised (for the most part) with the understanding that if someone does something for you, there are likely some expectations, and those expectations are usually pretty standard as they center around *gratitude* and *thanksgiving*. Yet we often see someone accept the gift of God's grace and abscond with it as if they earned, stole or were deserving of it, without ever stopping to consider what the expectations are.

In this chapter I hope to relay some of what I believe concerning those expectations and what is our reasonable service. To begin with, I would like to deal with the qualifying word in the key phrase that we are considering. The phrase, of course, is "which is your reasonable service," and the qualifying word is "reasonable." Reasonable, in this case, is an adjective, and it describes the object of the phrase, which is service, or more appropriately, your service.

Consider the Greek: the word "reasonable" is transliterated from "logos," which is familiar looking; it looks a lot like our English word *logical.* When we consult the Greek lexicon, we get an even better feel for the word; it is defined as "rational, sensible, true to real nature, pertaining to being genuine, or pertaining to mind and heart." We might also consider a couple of other versions and/or paraphrases; therein we see the phrase "your spiritual service" as seen in the ESV or "your spiritual service of worship" as seen in the NASB, or "your reasonable (rational, intelligent) service *and* spiritual worship" as seen in the AMP, which is of course a paraphrase.

Let's read the verse again. It is Romans 12:1, "I beseech you therefore, brethren, by the mercies of God, that ye present your bodies a living sacrifice, holy, acceptable unto God, which is your reasonable service."

Now allow me a little preacher's paraphrase of the Apostle Paul. *"Brothers, I am pleading with you, based upon all that I have shared with you concerning the power of the gospel, the spiritual needs of mankind, including the heathen, the gentile, and the Jew; and considering all that God has accomplished for us in Christ, how that He became sin for us, and now offers new life, no condemnation, and the status of more than conquerors, to all who will confess that He is Lord, and believe in their heart that God has raised Him from the dead; that you offer up your bodies, your literal lives not as a blood sacrifice, not as a dying sacrifice but rather as a living sacrifice, one that is Holy, one that is acceptable unto God, which is performed in and through your spiritual service, because this is sensible, it is reasonable, and it is logical that we would do this."*

Romans 12:1-2 is the type of passage that everyone has preached; it is a common charge passage, and it is as common as Hebrews 12:1-2, or the passages of note in Philippians 4. Also, this passage is rarely presented as a Church Body passage, but that is precisely what it is. If you will notice, the Apostle Paul would continue in the remainder of Romans 12 to discuss the Body and the member's place therein. He also discusses the individual members' attitude concerning themselves (wherein he states that they should not think more highly of themselves than is right), he deals with how we interact with one another, and he deals with unity as well in verse 16. So, we are certainly within the context of the Church.

So, we see that based upon all that God has accomplished, there is reasonable service, and there is an expectation. We should understand that this reasonable service is not some form of payment or obligation. It is not some type of payback or get-even. Instead, it is, or at least it should be, something that is done in light of the relationship. It is something we do for Him because He has done for us. It is not salvific, it does not provide some more righteous position for us because our righteousness is as filthy rags, and we are dependent upon the righteousness of Christ. Rather, this "reasonable service" is reflexive, reactionary, responsive, and reciprocal in form.

He loved us, so we love Him. He gave himself for us, so we give ourselves for Him. He died for us, so we live for Him.

In other words, it is not something we do to earn a spot in the Body; rather, it's something we do because we possess a spot in the Body. We don't love our children to win them as our children. We love them because they are our children. We do not seek to honor and care for our spouse hoping to convince them to become our spouse, but we honor and care for them because they are our spouse. You may believe I am belaboring the point. However, I am convinced that if we treated our children the way we treat our church family, someone would turn us into the Department of Family and Children's Services. And if we attended to the needs of our spouse the way many attend to the needs of the Body of Christ, the divorce rate would skyrocket. And that's saying something in today's marital climate.

A friend recently stated it this way. There are 52 Wednesdays in a year, and many church members never attend a Wednesday evening service. How would the typical spouse respond if you didn't come home 52 times in one year? I realize that sounds like the common country song, but the consideration is legitimate.

The Apostle Paul uses marriage as a type of Christ and the Church in Ephesians 5. We typically use this passage to teach about Christian family structure and healthy marriage relationships, and these applications are true, but since it is the case that the marriage is typical of Christ's relationship to the Church, then we can see some correlation to the individual believer's relationship to the church as well. We also know that God has ordained just three institutions, the oldest of which is marriage, second to that government, and lastly is the Church. Since we know that the Church is one of these three institutions, we should be interested in right relationship with it.

So, we are discussing the fact that for the Church to flourish in accordance with biblical expectation, it will require more than your service; indeed, it will require your sacrificial service. I believe that sacrificial service is what the apostle is referring to in Romans 12:1 when he mentions "your reasonable service." I believe this because of the request which is to "present yourself as a living sacrifice."

So, let's look first at the idea of service, and then we will consider how it becomes sacrificial. Notice the following passage.

Romans 12:3-21 says, "For I say, through the grace given unto me, to every man that is among you, not to think of himself more highly than he ought to think; but to think soberly, according as God hath dealt to every man the measure of faith. For as we have many members in one body, and all members have not the same office: So we, being many, are one body in Christ, and every one members one of another. Having then gifts differing according to the grace that is given to us, whether prophecy, let us prophesy according to the proportion of faith; Or ministry, let us wait on our ministering: or he that teacheth, on teaching; Or he that exhorteth, on exhortation: he that giveth, let him do it with simplicity; he that ruleth, with diligence; he that sheweth mercy, with cheerfulness. Let love be without dissimulation. Abhor that which is evil; cleave to that which is good. Be kindly affectioned one to another with brotherly love; in honor preferring one another; Not slothful in business; fervent in spirit; serving the Lord; Rejoicing in hope; patient in tribulation; continuing instant in prayer; Distributing to the necessity of saints; given to hospitality. Bless them which persecute you: bless, and curse not. Rejoice with them that do rejoice, and weep with them that weep. Be of the same mind one toward another. Mind not high things but condescend to men of low estate. Be not wise in your own conceits. Recompense to no man evil for evil. Provide things honest in the sight of all men. If it be possible, as much as lieth in you, live peaceably with all men. Dearly beloved, avenge not yourselves, but rather give place unto wrath: for it is written, Vengeance is mine; I will repay, saith the Lord. Therefore if thine enemy hunger, feed him; if he thirsts, give him drink: for in so doing thou shalt heap coals of fire on his head. Be not overcome of evil but overcome evil with good."

We could also consider Ephesians 4, 1 Corinthians 12, and Colossians 3-4 relative to the Body and the believer's position within it. We could consider 1 Thessalonians for some insight on the service of the individual believer. But we will confine our discussion for the time being to Romans 12.

In verse 6, Paul states that we have differing gifts and names several. This is not an exhaustive list, but we see some pictures of service within the body. Note that he mentions prophecy, teaching, ministry, exhortation, giving, ruling, merciful, cheerful, loving, kindness, self-deprecating, fervency, and enthusiasm. He also mentions rejoicing, hopeful, patient, prayerful, hospitable, honest, and humble.

These are all words that describe service to the Body. I realize that many of these may seem like emotions, but they are rather interactions with one another. These interactions often take on the air of service because they may help a fellow believer across some difficulty or through some tribulation. So that believers' service may be displayed in a connection between them and another brother and the way that they perceive his need and supply that need with a proper response. The antithesis to this picture of service would be found in the self-aware, self-concerned, self-motivated individual who is too self-occupied to share a rightfully perceived encouragement or exhortation.

The believer's service may take on a more utilitarian approach; he or she may become a teacher and may be able to encourage a classroom full of folks each week. Or their service may be to welcome and greet folks each week and in this ministry, they are allowed to express their hospitable side. They may be asked to lead a project for the pastor or for the Sunday School class so that, for the moment, they are ruling or leading and accepting the responsibility for the project.

There is literally an innumerable plethora of opportunities to serve. But you must be in attendance, in agreement, in abidance, and looking for an opportunity. I believe Coach Bob Green, the legendary football coach at Montana Tech, stated it best when he said that he desired his team to be "like a woodpecker in a petrified forest," stating that they should "just keep busy and look for opportunities." This is how the born-again believer should be at the local church. The Apostle Paul would state it this way. "Therefore, my beloved brethren, be ye steadfast, unmovable, *always abounding in the work of the Lord, forasmuch as ye know that your labor is not in vain in the Lord.*"

I suppose that sometimes there may be difficulty in discerning service opportunities within the local assembly. I am aware of several instances wherein I would have visitors attend my church, and they might attend several services, but the day would come when they were no longer attending. Upon several of these occurrences during my follow-up with them, they would say something like this, "Well, Pastor we loved the church, and we certainly enjoyed our time with you, but we didn't see a place that we could serve, we didn't think we could help your ministry, and so we went somewhere that needed our help." This is always quite disappointing because, indeed, we needed help, but the opportunities were not properly communicated. My point is, if you don't readily see a need or an opportunity, ask; because I can assure you there is a need.

We have considered the basics of service, but what about sacrificial service? How does that appear? How can it be applied?

I would remind you of our chosen definition of sacrificial, as found in Merriam-Webster's, which states it this way, "the destruction of or surrender of something for the sake of something else, or something given up or lost."

As it relates to service, I believe the idea of sacrifice is going to come from the raw and maybe gut-checking work ethic of the member. I apologize for such mundane and gritty-sounding words, but at times, this is what service within the Body feels like. It comes from the idea that someone must accomplish the work, and if I am the only one available, then *I* will make sure that the need is met. The antithesis of this would be to allow something to go undone because it isn't your job, your calling, or within your comfort zone.

The examples of unmet needs are innumerable. Just consider the nursery list with the same four names even though there are fifteen to twenty others capable of fulfilling nursery duty. You could see the same need often in the other volunteer children's ministry jobs. The various other consumer needs in the church that are often fulfilled by the same two or three volunteers, such as audio/video ministry, the greeter's ministry, the security team, and the parking lot crew. Often, this will lead to the complete burnout of a member, all because others would not accept some of the responsibility for the needs within the body.

The excuses are common and usually very difficult to argue with, even if leadership had the desire to debate. But at the root of most excuses is the lack of a sacrificial attitude as is relative to service within the body. But wouldn't this qualify as the "reasonable service" that Paul was speaking of? If we are indeed in Christ. And we are indeed a member of the Body. Shouldn't we have some responsibility within the Body, and wouldn't we expect that responsibility to be equally distributed among the members?

Maybe we should take a moment to dispel what I believe is a common misconception. Attendance, while desirable to the body and beneficial to the member, is not a form of service. In fact, attendance, under most circumstances, qualifies as being served rather than serving. Unfortunately, many have predetermined that faithfulness ends with attendance, when true faithfulness only begins in attendance.

There is also the regularity of attendance to consider; if the church meets on Sunday mornings, Sunday evenings, and Wednesday evenings, would we then consider someone who attends once per week to be a faithful member of the Body? If the church offers these three opportunities as well as Bible fellowship, Sunday school, or small groups, would we consider someone to be a faithful member who only attends Sunday morning worship? And we would withhold asking the same question concerning outreach and other special events.

So, we have stated that attendance is typically considered being served rather than service. However, if someone is faithful to attend all services and events, then there is certainly some level of personal sacrifice being experienced, and there is a calendar that has been captured by the Lord. In fact, I would be very excited to see a person or a family make this type of commitment because if they are fully immersed in the program of the church, and if the church is working expositionally through the scriptures, soon enough that family will be serving rather than being served. Indeed, if I had one recommendation to the believer it would be to find a church that you can totally immerse yourself in and watch the Lord work in your life.

One common objection that is offered towards any serving that supplants the morning worship is that the believer just can't spiritually afford to miss any worship service or preaching hour (security, nursery, children's church, preschool, etc.). This is one of those excuses that no one is willing to debate, and can you blame them? Who would want to be responsible for the spiritual well-being of another believer who is confident that they just cannot miss any of the preaching?

But might I suggest that if a member is faithfully involved in all or some of the other study and worship opportunities offered by the church, serving in another capacity would then become a cathartic experience during which they could express some of what they have learned, and they could exercise the "love for one another" that is so befitting of the born-again? And if you are fortunate enough to attend a church that offers multiple Sunday morning worship opportunities, there is no loss at all as you may well serve in one and attend the other.

We are considering sacrificial service. The thought process behind sacrificial service is, first, Body health and well-being, and second, community impact. Specifically, what is best for the Body, what will benefit the Church, and what is most profitable for the other attendees? What can I do that will make it easier for someone to hear the truth? What can I do that will make visitors more comfortable? What can I do that will result in the salvation of a child, a teen, a young adult, a mom, or a dad?

The sacrifice within the realm of service is primarily as it relates to time, schedule, or calendar. There is, of course, some self-sacrifice relative to the duty chosen and whether it is a strain on your personality or your comfort level, but these things usually pass with time, and we grow accustomed to the task and likely even come to enjoy them as the Lord gives His grace.

The schedule sacrifice is legitimate and truly one of the harder aspects for many, especially with the busier lives many lead today. And each person and/or family will need to consider the cost in this area. We have clear instruction, even from the Lord himself, as he spoke about taking up the cross, denying self, letting the dead bury the dead, forsaking father and mother, etc. Consider Matthew 19:29, "And every one that hath forsaken houses, or brethren, or sisters, or father, or mother, or wife, or children, or lands, for my name's sake, shall receive a hundredfold, and shall inherit everlasting life."

Nonetheless, this is a consideration and ultimately a commitment that must be made personally, or if there is a family involved, it must be agreed to by all the adults because if we are to place the church at the center of the calendar, there will be sacrifices, and there will be noticeable differences. But the benefits will far outweigh the difficulties, and the return on investment is otherworldly (pardon the pun). In my experience the benefits resulted in a closer family as well as a closer walk with the Lord. They also resulted in an expanded family in the church, a community within which we felt supported (again within the church), and a clear compass for family manners, child rearing, financial management, and marriage wellbeing. There were also personally realized benefits that many would likely associate with being born again. For me, they were elevated and accelerated due to the circumstances that I encountered while serving in various different and often difficult situations, which pushed me closer to the Lord, deeper in the Bible, and more devoted in prayer. And in truth, this all began with a simple commitment to attend and further commitment to serve.

I have witnessed this in others as well. I have observed entire family trajectories change based upon a commitment to attend. I have also witnessed good families struggle desperately while trying to satisfy the spiritual and the carnal, unable to make a real, lasting commitment to the Lord, and suffering from the problems of being double-minded, which the Bible states is unstable in all ways. One young father told me once that he had determined to be a yes man for the Lord. This thrilled my soul, and I have watched as the Lord has continued to work in his life.

I have also experienced a father and mother who are resistant to a total commitment to the church. They will usually speak of family time or family vacation; they will claim some type of protective activism over their camping or boating time as if these events have become venerated within their family. The more spiritually astute families will speak of family devotion, the family altar, and the family church as if the regular events of the Church interfere with these things. I have witnessed both types of families grow and as their children reach teen years and familial/parental communication becomes strained they need a spiritual partner to turn to that often does not exist because they have failed to develop a relationship with the Church.

There are also "faithful church families" that have difficulties with their teens and young adults, and I am in no way promising an escape from the difficulties of growing up in a fallen world, but I am saying that it is easier within a healthy church family.

In my experience the schedule is more of a rearranging and/or reorientation than it is a complete sacrifice. Sundays are easy, you just simply set them aside. Once you do this as a family, the whole unit will adapt to the new reality, and if mom and dad are sincere, the children will actually embrace the commitment that Sundays are for the Lord. Admittedly, Wednesdays are increasingly hard, with the continued secularization of society, and this includes the recreational leagues and the public-school leagues. People no longer regard Wednesday as a protected night, but arrangements can often be made if the family is sincere; and respect will usually be given. Special events are just that; they are special, and so they do not require a complete overhaul to the schedule but rather just an occasional adjustment.

It is necessary here to mention that I do not believe there is a sacred schedule prescribed in the Bible. No one has ever shown me, in the Scriptures, a set schedule for the church's gathering. I also understand that a cursory review of church history, and American history will prove any such proposal to be very shaky. I accept the exhortation in Hebrews 10:25, "Not forsaking the assembling of ourselves together, as the manner of some is but exhorting one another: and so much the more, as ye see the day approaching" as unto the Church. I appreciate the effort of many to maintain a traditional church attendance schedule. However, I am also aware of the earnest intentions of many churches to lower the expectations of thrice weekly attendance to increase the quality of gathering, even if it means decreasing the quantity. If the gospel is preached, the community is reached, the Body is served, and the disciples are growing, I have no complaints. The point of this book is not to define what is a healthy church methodology rather what is a healthy church member, and this member is dedicated and faithful to all the services and events of the local assembly to which they belong. They are fully committed.

There are very real enemies to this type of commitment. They will attack early and often. They will attack relentlessly. But if sincerity is expressed, and the Lord is sought, relief will come and victory with it.

There are absolute pitfalls to avoid, and they are controversial; they engender strife, but the believer who is committed to the body will recognize these things and avoid them. And when you make a mistake (and you will) and get involved in one of them, repentance will come, and with it restoration and resilience.

I am no longer raising children. I am a pastor, so most everyone knows where I stand. And lastly, I am not afraid of this type of controversy so I am going to list a few enemies that you should avoid if commitment and faithfulness to the church is your goal.

Any club and or organization that frequently meets on Sundays or Wednesdays. No matter what benefit is promised or perceived, if they do not respect the Lord's Day, you should avoid them. If they offer an alternative "church experience," they are simply telling you that they do not honor the Lord's Day. Travel teams, football, basketball, baseball, softball, dance, cheer, or anything else that is designed to perform or play away from home and specifically on the weekend. Even if they promise no Sunday events, they usually still interfere, even if it's just the distance or the fatigue from traveling all day on Saturday. All-star teams are usually designed to play on the weekend, and typically, they overlap on Sundays.

I realize that you just fell out of your chair. You think that I am suggesting robbing your children of all the fun things in life and stifling their creativity and athleticism. I also realize that this may seem out of touch or old-fashioned. The latter may be true, but I am not sure that it is a bad thing. Remember, we are discussing the ability to manage your schedule and be fully committed to the Church.

The suggestion is not to withhold your children from everything. Rather, it is to teach them and model for them an undeniable and uninterruptible dedication to the Body of Christ. And directly to the

Church, which is the Body of Christ. If they are a superstar athlete or dancer, God will honor this commitment and prosper their careers. If they are not a superstar, the recreation leagues and local competitions will be just as challenging and rewarding. But no matter their abilities and talent you will have taught them that their relationship with God is a first and foremost priority. While at the same time teaching them the biblical truth that a healthy relationship with God is expressed through a healthy relationship with the local Body of believers. Not to mention the muscle memory that you will create by attending every event, and every service, this will impact the way that they see the Church in the retrospect of their childhood. And while there may be a time when they drift from faithful, involved church membership, there will likely also be a time when they return to it.

The Mormon writer and radio broadcaster of the mid-20th century, Richard L. Evans, is quoted as saying, "Parents who indulge themselves 'in moderation' may have children who indulge themselves to excess." This was later colloquialized as, "What parents do in moderation, their children will do in excess," and this is how I have heard it stated most of my life. I believe this to be a truism based upon Scripture narratives concerning generational failure. I also believe it to be true based on personal and practical experience.

Of course, the negative is implied. For example, if the parent is moderately loving, we would not expect the child to be excessively loving because that would be counterintuitive to human nature, which is a fallen or sinful nature. Rather, if the parent is moderately loving, the indication is that they are also moderately disconnected, and then we would expect the child to be excessively disconnected.

Likewise, if the parent is moderately faithful to the Church, the implication is that they are also moderately uncommitted to the

Church, and so we would expect that child to have little or perhaps no desire for corporate worship or for the church proper because they witnessed it devalued by the actions of their parent(s). We could extrapolate the exemplification of this scenario, but I don't believe it is necessary; suffice it to say that your child is watching you, and whether or not they will ever admit it, their desire is to be just like you. Give them something good to aim for, show them how to be an integral part of the Body of Christ, show them a life lived for others, and show them what the true expectation of a coming Savior looks like. You will not be sorry.

To be clear, we all have regrets, we all have experiences that we wish we could relive and decisions that we wish we could remake. The goal is to minimize the regrets. The only way I know to do this is to be as immersed in the Word, and in the Body, and in the Life of Christ as is possible. Sacrificial serving is the supernatural outflow of this immersion.

Are you fully committed to the Body of Christ? Does your entire schedule revolve around the local assembly? Are you a sacrificially serving?

Father, thank you for loving us when we were unlovely. Thank you for God's mercies, the sacrificial substitutionary death of our blessed Savior, the Lord Jesus Christ. God, would you help us to know what our reasonable service is? Help us to know what you expect of born-again believers and help us to walk worthy of the vocation wherewith we are called. Amen.

Chapter Nine
The Hidden Treasures of Tithing and Giving

Once again, let's remind ourselves of the thesis for this project. For the (your) Church to function (this is basic), there must be selflessness, service, and financial support (this includes you), but if the Church would flourish and catch fire (this is biblical), significant sacrifice must be added. That means that your selflessness isn't enough; you must be sacrificially selfless. Your service isn't enough; it will require your sacrificial service. *And your financial support isn't enough; you must be sacrificially supportive.*

If this book has been difficult for you to agree with, it is likely about to become more difficult. If sacrificial selflessness is a challenge for you (as it is for most), then this chapter will be an even greater challenge. If you struggle with the idea of sacrificial service, then this chapter will likely also present a struggle. If your calendar or schedule is a hard sell, then I imagine that your checkbook will be an even larger commitment. But even with all these known challenges and struggles, we move forward with our thesis with the understanding that a church cannot function on the lighthearted commitment of lighthearted Christians.

A failed understanding of the biblical principles of giving is one of the greatest obstacles for many believers. As I have previously stated, I am convinced that born-again believers desire to do right, that is, to obey the word of God. And so, I believe that ignorance of the Word of God as it relates to giving is a great obstacle.

The false expectations that are associated with giving which have been created by false teachers, which fail to materialize (because they are false), is another great deterrent to biblical stewardship among faithful and semi-faithful church folk. The false promises range from blessings to wealth, from well-being to position, prominence, and power. There is a type of quid pro quo that is presented among many false teachers, which can be misconstrued as legitimate for a time but is always exposed and usually very hurtful to those who have been duped.

Lastly, faulty budget practices resulting in overbearing debt is likely one of (if not the) biggest threat to the Christian's desire to give biblically, and sacrificially. The fact is that by the time many Christians understand their financial responsibility, they have overspent and over-committed themselves with long- and short-term debt. And in their struggle to just "pay the bills" they find it seemingly impossible to honor God with their finances. And too often, by the time they are freed from the yoke of bondage to indebtedness, the burden to give has been overcome by a continual disobedience that was rooted in inability but is now habitual, and the conscience has become scarred to the conviction.

We will focus on these three issues in the next few pages. Failed understanding, false expectations, and faulty budget practices. A lack of understanding can be remedied with a pointed, applicable study of the Scriptures concerning the source of all wealth, the stewardship of the believer, and the single mind. Likewise, false expectations are a product of false teaching, which is the product of false exposition. This is usually centered on the greed of the purveyor, and a biblical comprehension of the eternal and the temporal, along with the above principles, should suffice in this revelation. Lastly, budget! Buckle up.

In my estimation, money, finances, and spending are among the greatest controversies in the church. Among the very few "disagreements" that I have had the displeasure of dealing with in the past twenty years, money was the scapegoat in most. I call it the scapegoat because it is often the go-to cover for other, more sinister issues, such as control, mastery, power, or prominence.

In fact, twice these issues centered around a proposed budget, which is money that is not even spent yet, because a budget is literally just a spending plan. Once, it revolved around a facility repair that was agreed upon by all and money that was already in the bank and earmarked for "maintenance." But the disagreement was over when to withdraw the money for the repair. My reason for bringing these situations up is not that we might adjudicate them and determine a winner. Rather, it is to merely reiterate the point that money and finances are divisive subjects and to simply ponder the question (Why?).

Why is it that money and finances are a divisive subject? Well, as I have already stated, it is relative to control, mastery, power, and prominence. This is why people often give to programs they agree with; it is so that they may express some control over the destiny of that thing. Conversely speaking, a person may withhold their donations to an organization if they do not agree with a certain decision, program, or plan. They may even express their disgust by saying, "I will not allow my money to be used for..." While I completely agree with this approach to secular organizations, it should not be so with the church and among the born-again believers. Because it is *His* church, and *His* plan, and we are *His* people.

As we have stated, a lack of understanding can be remedied with a pointed, applicable study of the Scriptures concerning the source of all wealth, the stewardship of the believer, and the single mind. We will spend some time with this in this chapter, but you should invest your own study time to consider the value of these truths.

In preview, allow me to summarize my beliefs in this area, and then we will look at some scripture for support. Since God is the creator and sustainer of all, and since He is sovereign over all, and since He has purchased me with the shed blood of His precious Son, He is the rightful owner of me and all that I possess. Without Him, I would be nothing, and without Him, I would have nothing, so all that I am and all that I have is because of Him. Therefore, whatever He requires of me or from me is acceptable since I belong to Him, and all I have belongs to Him. Furthermore, the church is His creation, it is His called-out assembly, and it has been given His commission. So, my involvement within the Church, to accomplish His will with my person and my possessions, is a foregone conclusion.

Let's consider first the source of all wealth. The word wealth can be subjective, depending upon culture and other implications. We might consider wealth to be opulence, abundance, or excess. But wealth can also simply mean any property with value, or anything with an exchangeable value. Your wealth may be greater than my wealth, but we both have wealth. So, we are not exactly speaking of abundance rather just the provision with which God has blessed you.

What is wealth? It is inclusive of all possessions whether great or small: housing, transportation, clothing, etc. In other words, you need not be wealthy or rich to possess wealth because whatever you possess is your wealth.

It is easy to get lost in today's culture. We see extreme opulence and extravagance, and we believe that is wealth, and we possess none of it. We see the outrageous contracts of professional athletes, entertainers and even the "influencers" on social media. Thirty years ago, the rage was all about millionaires. Today all we read about is the billionaires. We often say things like, "If I had a million dollars, I would..." Or we say "a billion? I would be satisfied with a cool million..." In this culture of affluence and excess, it is easy to begin to think that you don't have much or that you can't contribute much or enough to make a difference, but this is simply not true.

I have been blessed to travel to several foreign countries on short-term mission trips; I have visited Haiti four times, Peru, Jamaica two times, and spent a week in North Africa. Outside of seeing that the work of God is taking place in all these countries one of the greatest benefits for me was that of perspective. In Haiti, we worked in slums and in poor mountain villages; in Peru, we worked in shanty villages; in Jamaica, we worked among the poor communities; and in Africa, we visited with Berbers living in desolate high desert circumstances. I was once told that if you see one Third World situation, you've seen them all – and I agree that there is some truth to this. The similarity in all these places was the simplicity of life, the sparsity of possessions, and people's seeming contentment with what they had. We are accustomed to a pantry full of food; they have a day's worth of sustenance. We are accustomed to a cabinet full of dishes; they have a plate and a cup. We are accustomed to a closet filled with clothes; they have an outfit, and if they are truly fortunate, they have a Sunday coat. We have photo albums of the family, pictures, and décor on the walls. They are thankful if they have walls, and they may have one very special photo. Possessions and wealth are a matter of perspective.

On one particular trip, I was in Haiti. We were in the capital city of Carrefour, and we were traveling in several small trucks and vans. I was in the vehicle with the national pastor, and he was sharing certain details about the church in Haiti and the progress that was being made.

I noticed that along the side of the street, there was a continual stream of water. Along the way, there would be an occasional dog drinking from the stream, and then a child, and then sometimes an adult would bend down and fill their cup with that water. It was gray, and it certainly would have been devastating to one of us, suddenly I saw a lady on the street corner, and she was urinating in the stream of water... the same stream others were drinking from, before long another, and then a man, and then another child drinking from the stream. I was speechless; I could not believe what I was seeing. I didn't want to say anything because I was afraid I would hurt the pastor's feelings, and he didn't seem to notice; I wasn't sure anybody noticed except for me.

As I was processing what I was seeing, I witnessed this elderly lady standing beside that stream on a dirt hill. She had a broom in her hand and a set of bed sheets over her shoulder. In one quick movement, she unfurled those sheets onto that dirt hillside, and then she took a cup, dipped it into that gray water, and tossed it onto the sheets several times, and then she started scrubbing the sheets with the broom. I was absolutely overwhelmed, and before I could catch myself, I blurted out, "What is she doing!?" To which the pastor, a Haitian who had lived there all his life, responded, "She's washing her sheets." He said this rather incredulously as if to say, "Haven't you ever seen anybody wash their sheets before?"

This story has nothing to do with giving, but it has everything to do with perspective. It was a huge moment for me, because of the perspective that it gave. I am still grossed out by all the details, but the truth is that she wasn't aware of those frivolities; she simply needed to wash her sheets, and so she did. And I determined at that moment that a lot of what we get sidetracked with is just the frivolities of life, when we should just be looking at the facts at hand.

I may not be a millionaire or a billionaire; in fact, if I were liquidated, I would not even be a bad day on the market. But what I am is what God intended me to be, and what I have is what God intended for me to have, and I will seek to use it for His honor and glory.

The Bible is clear that all comes from the Lord. That is, everything comes from the Lord. He created it, He possesses it, He lends it, He multiplies it, and He can cause it to waste away. It is His. It is all His.

Abraham called God the Most High, the Possessor of Heaven and Earth (Genesis 14:19, 22). Moses said of the Lord that the Earth was His (Exodus 9:29, 19:5). The Psalmist had much to say about God's ownership.

We read various scriptures, and we are reminded of this fact. Deuteronomy 10:14, "Behold, the heaven and the heaven of heavens is the Lord's thy God, the earth also, with all that therein is."

Psalm 24:1, "The earth is the Lord's, and the fullness thereof; the world, and they that dwell therein."

Psalm 50:10, "For every beast of the forest is mine, and the cattle upon a thousand hills."

Psalm 74:16, "The day is thine, the night also is thine: thou hast prepared the light and the sun.

Psalm 89:11, "The heavens are thine; the earth also is thine: as for the world and the fullness thereof, thou hast founded them."

Psalm 95:4-5, "In his hand are the deep places of the earth: the strength of the hills is his also. 5 The sea is his, and he made it: and his hands formed the dry land."

Psalm 104:24, "O Lord, how manifold are thy works! in wisdom hast thou made them all: the earth is full of thy riches."

The Psalmist says that even vengeance belongs unto the Lord.

In the book of Job, we read that the Lord says the whole of Heaven is mine (Job 41:11). Jeremiah says that the day belongs to the Lord (46:10). Daniel says that wisdom and power belong to the Lord (2:20). Haggai records that the Lord says the silver is mine, and the gold is mine (2:8).

In his letter to the Colossians, Paul states that all things are created by Him, all things that are in Heaven and the Earth, visible and invisible, thrones, dominions, powers, and principalities, all created by Him. And in Him, all things consist, hold together, and/or remain. Everything that exists belongs to Him. All you have, all you are, all you may become...His. He is the source of all wealth.

Next, we will consider the stewardship of our wealth. We are still under the heading of false understanding. Hopefully, we agree that everything belongs to the Lord, which speaks to the source of our wealth. Now, let's take a moment to consider the stewardship of our wealth.

First, we should define stewardship; the Merriam-Webster dictionary states that stewardship is first the office, duties, and obligations of a steward, and second, it is the conducting, supervising, or managing of something, especially the careful and responsible management of something entrusted to one's care. The example given is that of our natural resources. We would understand this example because we can comprehend that they are not personally owned but they are personally managed or mismanaged depending on how someone interacts with them.

Part of the above definition is that stewardship concerns the office of a steward. Again, we would consult the Merriam–Webster dictionary and consider what a steward is. A steward is one employed in a large household or estate to manage domestic concerns (such as the supervision of servants, collection of rents, and keeping of accounts). Examples of a steward include a shop steward, a fiscal agent, an employee on a ship, airplane, bus, or train who manages the provisioning of food and attends passengers, one appointed to supervise the provision and distribution of food and drink in an institution, and one who actively directs affairs also known as a manager.

Just from these secular definitions, we should be getting a concrete idea about what or who a steward is and, likewise, what it means to steward the wealth that God has placed at your disposal. The thought is that of a manager, an agent, an overseer; it is a job and a responsibility. We are caretakers of another's goods and materials, and so if we spend them or use them frivolously, we are guilty of embezzlement or, at a minimum, a misappropriation of funds.

For depth and color, let's consider the biblical use of the term steward. The best Old Testament examples of a steward are found in the book of Genesis, in the person of Joseph, and then again in the book of Daniel, in the person of Daniel. In each case we see someone who is owned, Joseph was purchased for a price, and Daniel was taken as a spoil of victory, but both were the property of another, they had no rights of their own, they possessed no personhood or individuality as such so the decisions that they made were made on behalf of their masters and in consideration of what was best for their masters.

As we consider the New Testament passages connected with stewardship, we see several. We hear Paul describe his office as the office of apostleship, which is also the office of a steward.

Listen as he describes this responsibility 1 Corinthians 4:1-2

"Let a man so account of us, as of the ministers of Christ, and stewards of the mysteries of God. Moreover it is required in stewards, that a man be found faithful." And then again, the Apostle Paul speaking in Romans 14 about how we (the born again) should view one another, and he states that we are all servants, and that none of us live unto ourselves, but rather if we live we live unto the Lord and if we die we die unto the Lord. So then, whether we live or whether we die we are the Lord's. He concludes this comment with the admonition that we "each will give an account of ourselves unto God."

We would also consider the parables, and there are several that detail the interactions between a householder or a master and his stewards. In Matthew 25, the Lord shares the parable of talents, which deals with the stewardship of three servants and the use of the things entrusted unto them. We see a similar example in Luke 19 in the parable of Minas. Luke 12 shows the responsibility of servants and stewards toward the coming master. Again, Luke 16 deals with the unjust steward, or as some have termed it, the dishonest manager. Each of these passages paints for us a picture of stewardship, servanthood, the returning master, the reconciliation of gifts, and, in broad strokes, the responsibilities of every born-again believer as it is relative to the Lord.

We have been given the oversight of some wealth, possessions, or riches. These things are not ours to do with as we wish, but they are the Lord's, and they should be used to honor and glorify Him. This is accomplished by growing His kingdom, expanding His vineyard, or increasing His holdings.

To some extent, I have always viewed Luke 15 and the story of the lost son, or if you prefer, the prodigal son, as a picture of poor stewardship. I realize that this is not the optimum application, but there is some consideration of his inheritance that can be viewed as the gifts and abilities provided unto us by the Father. When we live selfishly and for the flesh, we are living riotously, immersed in the world, and in direct rebellion to the Father, and we are squandering our inheritance. But much like the promise made in the book of Joel, with repentance, God can restore the wasted years, the years devoured by the locust, the cankerworm, the caterpillar, and the palmerworm.

If we are born-again believers, then we are the servants of God; we are His doulos; we are His bond servants. And as such we have a responsibility to live our lives considering this truth. Furthermore, if He owns us, then He owns all that we own. Slaves do not maintain personal autonomy, and they do not maintain personal properties. We are His and everything we have is His. We may abscond with it and enjoy it selfishly but there will come a day when we stand before Him and give an account. Will we return His investment with growth? Will we return His investment with interest?

Will we return His investment unscathed but unprofitable? Or will we lose it all in riotous living and simply present ourselves covered in the filth of the world with nothing to show for it?

We must recognize the source of our wealth and be good stewards of all that has been entrusted to us. As we conclude this thought on a failed understanding, I would like to spend a moment in the book of Philippians and consider what Dr. Warren W. Wiersbe calls the "single mind."

In his book *Be Joyful*, Dr. Wiersbe states that although the keyword or theme in the book is joy (I believe it is used 19 times in the four chapters), the aim of the letter is to speak to us concerning the way we think, or our mind, or our attitude. He outlines the four chapters of the letter to the church at Philippi with a word describing how we think. He states that in chapter one, the "single mind" of the apostle is on display when he says, "For me to live is Christ and to die is gain". In chapter two, the "submissive mind" is on display in several examples but most prominently in the example of the mind of Christ, which we should all desire to have. In chapter three we see the "spiritual mind" as we are reminded of those who mind earthly things, and we are encouraged to know Him and the power of His resurrection. And lastly, in chapter four, we find a "secure mind" that is dependent upon the riches of God for all its needs.

Each of these mindsets should impact the way we perform as stewards of God. We should be single-minded in our focus; this life is not about me. It is about Christ and how I can glorify Him. We should have a submissive mind, think of others first, and esteem others better than ourselves; ask how we can use the wealth that God has given us to make sure others hear the gospel and have a chance to know God. In this chapter, Dr. Wiersbe makes the following comment. "If you love your things, you will use people to keep them, but if you love people, you will use your things to reach them!" We should have a spiritual mind so that we are always thinking of heaven and our citizenship therein, and we are always watching for the return of the Lord, ready to give an account. Lastly, we can have a secure mind, knowing that all good things come from God and that if we use our possessions to honor God, we can depend upon His riches in glory to fulfill all our needs.

Hopefully, now we understand (and agree) that the source of our wealth is the Lord, and our responsibility is to steward that wealth with a single mind.

The second issue, which often makes the subject of money and finances so divisive, is false expectations created by false teachers, who practice false exposition and improper differentiation between the temporal and the eternal.

There is a great deal of false teaching in the world concerning the Bible in general; these false teachings are often relative to salvation, security, spiritual giftings, and finances. The false promises range from personal blessings to private wealth. There are guarantees of well-being, desires for position and prominence, and even expectations of power. Many false teachers present a type of quid pro quo, wherein if you do this, then God will do that.

These false promises can be misconstrued as legitimate for a time, due to circumstance and coincidence, but in the end, they are exposed and usually very hurtful to those who have been duped.

The tragedies of financial failure in these so-called ministries, the opulence of supposed pastors and evangelists, contrasted with the typical poverty of those who give to these organizations, create a public spectacle. It tarnishes ministries worldwide and creates an air of suspicion, which folks will then use as an excuse to refrain from giving because "you can't trust organized religion."

To some degree, I understand this general distrust. When I see certain men living in multi-million-dollar mansions, flying around in corporate jets, wearing ultra-expensive clothing, or just living in an excessive manner, I am also offended. When I see men build multi-campus facilities and broadcast themselves like television hosts in various locations or helicopter between those locations for appearances, I am not reminded of the scriptures. I don't associate them with the good history of evangelism and soul winning, or of the circuit riders, or of anything remotely close to biblical Christianity and the local assembly. All I see is money, performance, power, prestige, notoriety, fame, and recognition. None of these things reflect servanthood, stewardship, or being a bondservant. And I think that they damage the public perception of the real work that God has called us to do.

We also must contend with the prosperity gospel that many of these same perpetrators are preaching. These promises of health and wealth. These promises of a quid pro quo relationship between the giver and God. These promises that, by and large, never come to fruition. It is a type of gambling wherein the hope is to invest a little and reap a lot. This is antithetical to all that the scriptures teach, love not the world nor the things of the world, no man can serve two masters, you can't serve God and mammon, lay not up for yourselves treasure on Earth where rust and moth doth corrupt, where your treasure is there your heart will be also. It is also a perversion of the things that are important, the things that truly matter. If this world is not my home, if indeed I am only passing through, why should God enrich me here in houses and lands? So, what do the scriptures teach concerning our giving? Or our financial support? Let's investigate that for a moment.

The issue of tithing and/ or giving to the church seems to be well debated and oft resisted. My suspicion is that it is debated and resisted for mostly the wrong reasons, and those reasons would center on selfishness: folks' desire to keep and spend their money as it seems fit to them without the Church, the Bible, or God being involved.

There are two forms of giving mentioned in the scriptures: the first is tithing, and the second is offerings. I believe they are both very applicable to the born-again believer, but if you are looking for this in the form of a New Testament commandment, something that is carved in stone, something akin to the two great commandments uttered by the Lord Jesus, upon which all of the other commandments hang; then I am sad to report to you that it is not available.

However, I have never heard an argument based on scriptures that has removed my conviction to give both tithes and offerings to God through the local assembly. Rather, each time I have visited this subject, I have come away convinced that every believer should participate in this system of support for God's work.

In fairness, if there were no scriptures that even mentioned giving, whether tithes or offerings, I would be easily convinced from a logical position of the need to give because I see value in the work that is being performed by the Church. We need a place to gather; we need this place to have similar comforts to other gathering venues; we need caretakers for these gathering places, and we need people who are well-versed in the sharing of the truths that we commonly believe. Based upon these needs alone, we could justify the necessity of giving.

Thankfully, there are scriptures that establish a method of giving that God will honor. When we observe these principles, He will bless both the gift and the giver so that all needs are met.

The first giving principle in the scriptures is the principle of the tithe. The term tithe literally means "tenth" in the Hebrew language. The tithe is established very early in the scriptures; in fact, it is established even before the Levitical/Aaronic priesthood is developed. We see the details of this occurrence in the book of Genesis and specifically in chapter 14, verses 18-20, which state, "And

Melchizedek king of Salem brought forth bread and wine: and he was the priest of the most high God. And he blessed him, and said, Blessed be Abram of the most high God, possessor of heaven and earth: And blessed be the most high God, which hath delivered thine enemies into thy hand. And he gave him tithes of all." The book of Hebrews describes this event in chapter 7, verses 1-10, as the writer builds his case for the preeminence of the High Priesthood of Christ. This is one of several New Testament passages that address the fact of the tithe and never is it annulled or done away with. Not once is it replaced with a better option or a new commandment.

Some will argue that this is an Old Testament practice that is done away with in the New Covenant, but I find no validation for that in the scriptures. The tithe and the act of tithing is very common throughout the Old Testament, and I could lay in many verses for you to read, but I would encourage you to simply pick up the Bible and read it for yourself and see how often it comes up. One website stated that it occurs 38 times in the Old Testament, which is pretty often considering that there are only 39 Old Testament books.

If we are curious as to how God views tithing, we need to look only so far as the little book of Malachi. Within the pages of Malachi, four short chapters, the last of the prophets, and the last book of the Old Testament, there is a scathing rebuke for many of Israel's failures. William MacDonald's *Believers* Bible Commentary uses the following words in his outline of this little firebrand of prophecy. He states that Israel is guilty of ingratitude, sacrilege by the Priest, divorce and mixed marriages, denial of God's Holiness and Justice, backsliding of the people, robbing God of tithes, and making false charges against God.

In chapter 3, verses 8-12, the prophet asks the question and provides God's perspective of the tithe. "Will a man rob God? Yet ye have robbed me. But ye say, Wherein have we robbed thee? In tithes and offerings. Ye are cursed with a curse: for ye have robbed me, even this whole nation. Bring ye all the tithes into the storehouse, that there may be meat in mine house, and prove me now herewith, saith the Lord of hosts, if I will not open you the windows of heaven, and pour you out a blessing, that there shall not be room enough to receive it. And I will rebuke the devourer for your sake's, and he shall not destroy the fruits of your ground; neither shall your vine cast her fruit before the time in the field, saith the Lord of hosts. And all nations shall call you blessed: for ye shall be a delightsome land, saith the Lord of hosts." I think that is clear and needs no qualification. The tithe belongs unto God, as does all that we are and all that we have.

The next giving principle mentioned in the scripture is the offering. Also known as the free-will offering, the gift is given freely and from the heart of the giver as they are so moved, often by the blessed Holy Spirit. This is a gift over and above the tithe. We see this idea of offering in the collection of materials for the construction of the tabernacle in the wilderness. In Exodus 25:1-8, "And the Lord spake unto Moses, saying, Speak unto the children of Israel, that they bring me an offering: of every man that giveth it willingly with his heart ye shall take my offering. And this is the offering which ye shall take of them; gold, and silver, and brass, And blue, and purple, and scarlet, and fine linen, and goats' hair, And rams' skins dyed red, and badgers' skins, and shittim wood, Oil for the light, spices for anointing oil, and for sweet incense, Onyx stones, and stones to be set in the ephod, and in the breastplate. And let them make me a sanctuary; that I may dwell among them." There is a second appeal for this offering in Exodus chapter 35, and then in Exodus 36:5-7 we read, "And they spake unto

Moses, saying, The people bring much more than enough for the service of the work, which the Lord commanded to make. And Moses gave commandment, and they caused it to be proclaimed throughout the camp, saying, Let neither man nor woman make any more work for the offering of the sanctuary. So, the people were restrained from bringing. For the stuff they had was sufficient for all the work to make it, and too much." We see other free will offerings throughout the Old Testament usually associated with the work of the Lord, or the House of God. We also see it in relation to the return from captivity in Ezra.

As we enter the New Testament, we would consider the book of the Acts of the Apostles, and in it, we see some examples of free will offerings (Barnabas, Ananias, and Saphira). Also, we would consider the writings of the apostle Paul, wherein he instructs that an offering be taken for the collection of the saints. He would specifically instruct the Church at Corinth to "Upon the first day of the week let every one of you lay by him in store, as God hath prospered him, that there be no gatherings when I come."

In my opinion, the tithes and offerings are well established in the scriptures as a part of New Testament Christian life. I think the arguments over whether I am responsible or whether I must give tithes and offerings are akin to all of the other fruitless conversations we have concerning what I can and can't do (must or mustn't do) as a born-again believer. The Apostle Paul says, "All things are legal, but not all things are expedient." I think we can rightly ascertain that I can withhold my tithes and offerings if I choose to, but it certainly is not expedient for the Church, and it is not expedient for my spiritual growth, nor does it reflect obedience unto God, which is Christ-likeness; "Let this mind be in you, which was also in Christ Jesus: Who, being in the form of God, thought it not robbery to be equal with

God: But made himself of no reputation, and took upon him the form of a servant, and was made in the likeness of men: And being found in fashion as a man, he humbled himself, and became obedient unto death, even the death of the cross." (Philippians 2:5-8)

Imagine if all the born-again believers in the Church were tithing faithfully and giving free-will offerings. Let's just play with a little math. At the writing of this book, according to the county census, the median household income in my county is listed as $81,434.00. The study also states that the average household is comprised of 2.9 people.

If a church had a membership of 225 then that would represent about 80 households, not counting visitors. If these 80 households met that median income and they all tithed on their income the church tithe base would be $650K. Even if only about 70% of the members were considered active, the tithe base would still be $447K. These membership numbers and attendance rates are a close match to the church I currently pastor. We are a healthy church, a vibrant church, a church other churches look up to, and yet our tithe base is still less than $350K, for which I am very thankful and maybe even a little proud, but the fact remains that there is a significant differential in those numbers. What could we do for the Lord, for missions, for members, for the community, with another $100K? What could we do with another $300K?

I challenge you to look at these figures in relation to your church and ask the same questions. Then ask yourself: Am I tithing? Am I giving free-will offerings? Remember the question the Lord asked the exiles in Haggai, "Is it time for you to dwell in your ceiled houses, and this house (His house) lie waste?"

Lastly, in this chapter, I want to deal with the third and possibly greatest reason that believers fail to tithe and participate in free-will offerings. Remember, reason one was a failed understanding of wealth, reason two was false expectations based upon false exposition, and reason three is faulty budget practices.

Budget practices may feel personal, and the conversation may seem intrusive, but fortunately, I'm not sitting with you at your kitchen table or mediating the conversation between you and your spouse.

And I am not sharing anything that you're not already aware of at some level. And I am not claiming any personal high ground because if we are honest, we have all had these struggles and may have them again. What I am about to share with you is common knowledge and well-covered in several financial help books.

The reason that many well-meaning, otherwise obedient Christians do not tithe is that they have a poorly managed budget, and they have either accrued too much monthly debt or they simply spend everything that they make before they get around to tithing. My father has always said that you can't get blood out of a turnip; he also commonly says, "That's the thing about money: once you spend it, it's gone!" So, when a believer becomes convicted about tithing or giving extra if they don't have it, they can't give it, and if the "don't have it" is a chronic problem of outstanding debt, it may take a while to get things in the right order. But regardless of your circumstances, it is very wise to pursue the proper tithe.

I recently heard one of the smart money gurus tell churches to back off so that people could get on their feet and then they could start tithing. I am not sure how to feel about that. While I am not a proponent of churches commanding folks to tithe, billing them for their tithe, or examining their W2 to set the tithe (all horror stories that

I have heard along the way), neither am I comfortable with a money manager speaking to churches as if he has some level of authority over them. Tithing is biblical. Tithing is discipleship. Tithing should be taught, and it should be preached when the passage permits it. This is the church's duty, this is the pastor's duty, and it is the teacher's duty.

Allow me to restate that teaching tithing is the church's, the pastor's, and the teacher's duty. It is not their duty to mandate, legislate or enforce it as if it were some code.

For the believer, tithing is a matter of obedience, conviction, and personal responsibility. Just like your calendar should revolve around your church attendance, so should your budget revolve around your tithing. This book is not a financial planning manual, but suffice it to say if your budget will not allow you to tithe, you are over-extended and need to seek the Lord's forgiveness, followed by the Lord's wisdom in how to repair your finances to a place where you can tithe, and by all means, begin giving as soon as possible, and do so consistently, until such time as you can actually tithe.

There is yet another objection that I have heard on several occasions that I will address here, and then we will close this chapter. The argument is always an appeal to better sense, and it usually includes an objection to the way the money will be spent. There are several ways for the tither to overcome this problem. First, if you don't like the way the money is managed, then you should attempt to get involved and help manage it in a manner that seems right to you. Second, if you are not allowed any input into the way the money is spent, and you cannot come to an agreement with the way the money is spent, then you are at the wrong church. You should depart posthaste and find yourself another church whose spending habits you agree with. Lastly, if you are not or cannot be involved in the decision-making process, or you don't want to be in the decision-making process, your responsibility of the tithe ends with the giving. In other words, you will not be held accountable for how that money was used; the leaders will. You will only be held accountable for your obedience in giving it. I find that even this argument is typically an excuse.

So, as we close this chapter, let's remember that we said your financial support is not enough; it will require sacrificial financial support. That simply means that your entire budget revolves around your tithe and offerings. The tithe comes out first, and then the budget is managed to its completion. If there is a windfall of money, it should certainly be tithed upon, but there is also the consideration of free will offerings; maybe it should be given, or a portion given in order to help the church with a special project. I cannot count the times as a pastor when I have been praying about a need or a project within the church that we lacked the budget for and the Lord would send in a check from someone who had a burden to help, or simply appreciated the church ministry, or in memory of someone, or in honor of someone, and many times that would allow the church to accomplish the project when it otherwise could not have.

One time specifically, we were preparing to take a six-man mission team and smuggle some Christian materials into a closed country to a missionary who was in need. I stood the team up in front of the church and explained what we were going to do. I explained that it would be dangerous, rigorous, and expensive. I explained that we would all be raising the funds needed and the total for the team would be $10K dollars. We prayed together and dismissed the meeting. As I was walking to the rear of the church to greet visitors, a gentleman approached me and said that he had been visiting and that he wanted to write me a check to help with the mission trip, and he asked me how to make the check out. In just a moment, he handed me a check for $10K. The team was fully paid for, and we didn't need to raise any funds; we could focus on prepping for the trip. This man never joined, and to my knowledge, he has never given another dime to the church, but he was there when we needed him, and God used him to bless six families, a missionary family, and no telling how many believers and new converts over the life of those materials.

God wants you to be obedient and use the money that He has blessed you with to accomplish the work of the church. Will you obey?

Father, thank you for loving me and for giving me the opportunity to participate financially in the church. Lord, I confess there have been times when I have not given. Lord, I confess there have been times in my life when my budget would not allow me to give. Lord, I come now repenting of my failure and asking you to help me arrange my entire budget around my tithes and offerings. Lord, help me to be obedient in all that I do.

Chapter Ten
What Your Church Really Needs

The three previous chapters have attempted to define sacrificial, as in sacrificial selflessness, service, and financial support. We could have simply stated that we were defining sacrificial Christianity, which I believe is the same thing as uncommon membership in the church.

In Chapter 5, we discussed the megachurch movement and its impact on local churches, which eventually closed. They closed because there were not enough body members to keep the church functional. In fact, the distinction is made that the churches did not close for lack of facilities or pastors but rather for a lack of attendees —Christians who are born-again and are willing to do the work of the church.

The obvious result is fewer local churches, and we can say fewer smaller churches and fewer volunteer-fueled churches. This impacts the entire community, and the impact is generational. And it's not just fewer churches, but its fewer pastors in the community, fewer Sunday School teachers in the community, fewer deacons in the community, less church family, and less connection between our everyday lives and the church. And for all the jokes about preachers, deacons, and their children, something genuine is lost, and it is changing the community much the same way that big retail has.

I also shared in Chapter 5 the experience that I had as a local pastor on the funeral director's list and the number of services I performed for members of these large multi-campus churches. I was recently sitting in the waiting area of a local Longhorn's steakhouse; my wife and I were waiting at a table when the older gentleman across the way started a conversation with me. We talked for a moment about the long wait, the reduced staff, and other issues related to the recent pandemic. He then made a joke about the government and proceeded to tell me about a car accident he and his lady friend had recently been involved in. The conversation rambled about, and he let out that he was a retired pastor. I acknowledged that I was also a pastor, and we swapped cordials. I asked him how he kept himself busy, and he readily said, "Funerals. I performed over 80 last year." He went on to explain that he had gotten connected with a local funeral home and that they were calling him continually, sometimes two or three times a week. He even quipped that he recently did a "Catholic funeral" and he said, "I'm not even a Catholic!" What he said next confirmed what I have been saying in these last few paragraphs. My wife asked him why he thought that he was called so often, and he answered, "Thirty years ago, these people all moved out here, they bought a house, found a good school for their kids, and good job for themselves, but they didn't find a church, and now they don't have a pastor or a church family."

There was a time when the local church performed so many duties in our lives. The pastor was there if you went to the hospital, but now there is a paid, professional chaplain provided by the hospital, who doesn't know you or your family or your needs. The pastor was there when someone died, whether tragically, accidentally, or of natural causes, there he was to comfort the family, to reassure, to help with funeral arrangements, someone who knew the deceased, who understood their importance within the family, but now this role is filled by checking another box on the funeral directors' form, Catholic or Protestant. There was a time when a young man and young woman were ready to marry, and they would go to their pastor and plan the wedding in the church, and this man who had dedicated them as infants to the Lord as the church looked on, led them to the Lord, ministered to their family, likely baptized them both, and watched them mature would help them move into the next phase of life, under the watchful eye of a loving church family. In our current society, we hire a wedding coordinator, and we rent a wedding venue, and we choose a wedding officiant, and it is yet another professionally performed event with limited spiritual significance. There is no doubt that we need the local church. The community is better with the local church, but what does the church need? Can it be the church without you? Can it be the church without many of you? Do we really want to hire the church out as well?

In this chapter, I will seek to answer the question, "What does your Church need from you?"

The short answer is that your church needs you to *pair* up and get connected. By this, I mean that your church needs you to be *present*, which speaks to your attendance, spiritually and physically. Your church needs you to be *available.* This speaks to your service and your work within the church and community. Your church needs you to be *invested (*functionally and financially*)* in the current needs of the church, as well as the future of the church. The church needs you to be *resolute* in your commitment to Christ and to His Body, the Church.

When we think of being present, we must first consider your attendance. We have spent some time discussing your attendance in Chapter 6, wherein we defined it, not as your service but when you are served. Over the next couple of pages, we will seek to detail some of the benefits of your attendance—benefits to you personally, to the pastor, and to the Church proper.

First, consider some of the personal benefits of regular, faithful, committed church attendance. Habitual development is one aspect of good that comes from regular attendance. By this, I mean it sets your schedule habitually around the Church, and after a short while, this schedule then becomes fully natural: you expect it, your spouse expects it, your children expect it, and your friends and relatives expect it. Everyone knows when you will be in church, so there are fewer and fewer discussions about where you will be at any given time because you and everyone else know that you will be at the church. Before we attempt to make this a bad thing or an odd thing, I would encourage you to note the other habitual aspects of your life and the lives of others around you.

Your bedtime is probably habitual, the kid's bedtime is most likely habitual, your grocery schedule is likely habitual, your lawn mowing schedule is likely habitual, many folks have a habitual gym schedule, and the school calendar is habitual from year to year. I could make this point to a redundant and obnoxious end but suffice it to say that most people have some habitual tendencies. I am suggesting that church attendance should and could easily be one of them.

The next personal advantage that comes from being present (attendance) is helpful. It is the reality of spiritual growth. Most pastors that I know are preaching and teaching purposefully. By that, I mean there is an underlying, programmed intention to their body of work. For example, your pastor may always preach a gospel sermon with a strong evangelistic theme on Sunday mornings, and then on Sunday evenings, he may preach towards committed Christian living, and then on Wednesday evenings, he may preach/teach towards individual spiritual growth and maturity. If this is the case, and you only attend Sunday mornings, then all you ever hear is a gospel plea. If you are already born-again, you may become anemic in your Christian walk because all you ever hear is an appeal to get saved. You may even start thinking that this is all your pastor knows, "He says the same thing week after week, I just never get anything from his sermons." Well, the problem is that you are only hearing one-third of his weekly presentation.

Admittedly, not every pastor, church situation or church schedule is the same. But whatever the full schedule of the church is, if it is a church that is committed to the discipleship and spiritual growth of the individual Christian, it will appear only in the full schedule.

Imagine this same scenario with a different application. What if your child decided that they did not want to attend the full schedule of school? What if they determined that they would only go to the first two periods of each day? Then, when someone asked them what they were learning in school, they said, "Well, all my school teaches is basketball and math. They talk about the same thing every time I go. It's boring, I don't feel as if I am being taught." Is the school at fault? Or is the student responsible to be present for all the classes so that they will be a well-rounded scholar?

Consider the local restaurant, open six days a week, from 7:00 a.m. until 9:00 p.m. daily. But you only go at 9 am, every time you go, they are serving breakfast and every time you get pancakes and sausage. And then someone asks you what you think about the local restaurant. And you say, "Well, it's pretty good, but they have a limited menu; in fact, all they serve is breakfast." Is this a true statement? Or is it a perspective that is limited by your exposure to the restaurant?

I believe we can see the reality of these two scenarios and how they represent the idea of being present for all the learning opportunities at the church. I would encourage you to speak with your pastor and ask him to share his vision concerning the church program or the schedule by which he preaches. Allow me to reiterate that every church and each pastor is different. Also, church schedules can be different, but the program can and should still be complete and inclusive.

As an example, I will explain the schedule I currently use and show a couple of possible alternatives.

We operate a traditional format; by that, I mean that we offer a Sunday school for all ages, Sunday morning, Sunday evening, and Wednesday evening church. My focus as the pastor is on the morning and two evening events. Our Sunday school is age graded for the school ages. The adult Sunday school is divided by a hybrid of age, stage of life, and style of teaching. The Sunday school is unified in style of operation but not in curriculum; at the adult age, we allow our teachers to exercise their spiritual gifting and teach as they are guided, so that some use quarterlies, some use expositional study guides, and others just go directly to the Bible. But the point is that it is not synchronized.

The remainder of the services are synchronized and programmed to the extent that I will preach expositional series on Sunday mornings that are aimed at challenge, charge, conviction, and conversion. On Sunday evenings, I will preach expositional series that are aimed at Christian living, spiritual walk, or spiritual growth. At other times, we use Sunday evenings to present two to three classes per quarter that are intentional learning blocks. We call these focus groups. They are led by handpicked individuals, who are very qualified, and typically former pastors. We offer subjects such as dispensations, great doctrines of the faith, church history, and discipleship training; all these classes are set up on a 16-week semester; they have a syllabus, an outline, and handouts for each class. This provides for specific teaching, growth, and learning on an intentional schedule. Then, on Wednesday evenings, I will preach an expositional series towards the end desire of biblical knowledge, or leadership, or soul winning, a specific area that God has laid on my heart as being needed within the body.

So, if an individual is faithful to all the church services, they are receiving a well-rounded diet of evangelism, exposition, edification, exhortation, and education. If we needed to change the schedule, we could simply replace one of the evening services by becoming more intentional in the Sunday school hour.

So, being present develops habits in our schedule, is helpful to our spiritual growth, gives heart to the shepherd, and honors God. The pastor is the shepherd, and at times the shepherd can lose heart. We should not, but sometimes the battle just seems to be impossible. Society rages, Satan roars, and the family is attacked, and at times it looks as if we are losing ground. The old saying is that the pastor always quits on Monday, but I quit less on Monday when we have a fuller house on Sunday evening. And lastly, your presence in attendance is honoring to God, it is a small act that speaks a loud word of commitment unto the cause of Christ.

The second aspect of being present is your attention. That is, you are there in body, mind, and spirit. I would not suggest that someone could maintain a presence of attendance and not possess a presence of attention. Rather if we allow our attention to drift, soon our attendance will follow. I suppose the question is how we maintain our presence of attention, and I propose the answer is that we stay interested in spiritual things. This means that we should, as Christians, read the scriptures daily and, as students, exercise our minds in other areas that complement our Christianity. One way that I seek to help folks with this is that I prescribe a Pastor's Reading List. It is typically themed to match my sermonic direction and thoughts for the upcoming year. It will include a Bible reading schedule, as well as a monthly book suggestion. If members of the church follow this list (to the best of their abilities), they are more likely to maintain a presence of attention.

Lastly, in the arena of presence is the presence of affection. We must maintain a presence of affection for the other members of the Body in which we are practicing and for the members of the community in which we are participating. We could easily find these types of exhortations in the scriptures, "let each esteem others, better than self," and "Love your neighbor as yourself," but if we fulfill these desires, we must be present in our affections.

So, we must be present, in attendance, attentive, and affectionate. Next, we must be available, and as we have previously stated, this availability speaks of your service within the church and within the community.

We could likely divide this idea of availability into three areas of focus, we must be available for ministry and management within the church and for mission within the community.

We would look first at the idea of your service or your ministry within the church. This is a very broad field. There are opportunities as varied as personalities within most churches. To name a few, we could start with ushers, greeters, choir, sound and video, parking lot crew, security crew, Sunday school teachers, nursery workers, children's church workers, preschool children's church workers, children's club workers. The list is filled with opportunities for all types of folks.

Next, we think of management within the church, and of course we are considering the leadership positions in the church that require dedicated, qualified people. Positions such as finance, trustees, Sunday school director, youth director, children's director, etc. Often these jobs are performed by someone who is not a leader; they have a burden but not the God-granted skill. Other times the leaders in the church end up performing multiple jobs, and we see the Pareto principle in action, wherein 20% of the people perform 80% of the work. Both scenarios are the result of a lack of availability.

Lastly, as it relates to availability, we consider our community. There is a false impression among Christians that the Great Commission was given only to the church; it is the church's responsibility, and that we are failing in fulfilling the Great Commission because the church is failing. Let's look at the Great Commission and consider some context.

Matthew records the Great Commission in a very robust manner. Matthew 28:19-20, "Go ye therefore, and teach all nations, baptizing them in the name of the Father, and of the Son, and of the Holy Ghost: Teaching them to observe all things whatsoever I have commanded you: and, lo, I am with you always, even unto the end of the world. Amen."

Mark removes some of the details, but the message is the same. Mark 16:15-16, "And he said unto them, go ye into all the world, and preach the gospel to every creature. He that believeth and is baptized shall be saved; but he that believeth not shall be damned."

It is worded differently in the gospel of Luke, but again the message is the same. Luke 24:46-48, "And said unto them, thus it is written, and thus it behooved Christ to suffer, and to rise from the dead the third day: **47** And that repentance and remission of sins should be preached in his name among all nations, beginning at Jerusalem. **48** And ye are witnesses of these things."

John does not record the details of the Great Commission, but these words of Jesus are all of the motivation and definition that we need to apply ourselves unto the work. John 20:21, "Then said Jesus to them again, Peace be unto you: as my Father hath sent me, even so send I you."

In fact, even if we did not possess the Great Commission, we could establish that our great mission is defined in the life of Christ. Just as He was sent, we are sent from the Father as the light, with the truth, and in love to find those who are in the dark and lost.

Lastly, we see Acts 1:8, "But ye shall receive power, after that the Holy Ghost is come upon you: and ye shall be witnesses unto me both in Jerusalem, and in all Judea, and in Samaria, and unto the uttermost part of the earth."

This book is obviously not an exposition on the Great Commission, but we can see in the passage in Matthew a *procedure* for accomplishing the mission, namely that we are to teach, baptize, and disciple among all nations. We also see a *promise* of His *presence* with us as we do. And then in Acts, we see the *priority*, we are to be witnesses unto Him, we see the *plan*, that is at home and abroad (*both and at the same time*), we see the *power* which is the blessed Holy Spirit who indwells the believer and equips them for the work. And most importantly we see the *personnel* responsible for the carrying out of this plan, it is you and me.

The Great Commission was not given only to the church proper; rather, it was given to the believer, to the disciples, and to the individual. The Church may be the agency through which the commission is achieved, but the agent is the Christian or the believer.

So, as we consider the third aspect of your availability, which is your mission within the community, we would consider ways in which you, as an individual believer, a Christian, and an agent of the local church, are fulfilling the Great Mandate, which is the Great Commission.

The question is, "In what ways can the individual believer fulfill their mission? The answer: join the I team: invest, invite, invoke, intercede, include, and insist.

Every born-again believer should be investing in the mission work of the local church. That means that you are financially invested in the mission's outreach of your church. There are several ways to do this. You can give offerings over and above your tithe and ask the church to invest them in particular missions' opportunities that have already been identified as needy. You can participate in your church's annual Faith Promise campaign and do so in a faithfully significant way, or you can personally support missions through relationships outside of the church but meaningful in the community.

Every born-again believer should be inviting their family, friends, neighbors, and coworkers to church; they should do so until they are convinced that those individuals are involved with another like-minded church or until the Lord removes the burden for that person. Admittedly, this can become a tedious situation, and I don't recommend losing relationships, but there is a loving and non-nagging way to keep this invitation open and fresh.

Every born-again believer should pray regularly, invoking God to save those around them who display no fruit or signs of salvation. We should also daily intercede for our friends and family and for the missionaries we know who are facing the lost masses and sharing the good news with them.

Lastly, every born-again believer can participate in the missions and evangelistic work of their church. They should also insist on being trained and educated to accomplish these tasks.

The believer should be present and available, and then they should be invested in the work of the local assembly. How does this investment appear? It may appear in the form of manpower or money, but both are necessary for the church to flourish, which is biblical.

Let's look at the manpower aspect first; we have spoken about the possibilities for service and the diversity of possible personalities that can serve comfortably. I would like to spend a moment or two on manpower management.

Manpower management is a term that I have been hearing since I was a teenager. I love the sound of it and the thoughts that it provokes. It was first introduced to me as a military term by one of my older brothers. He was in the Air Force, and he was a manpower management specialist. I remember as a teenager asking him what that meant, and he said, in an off-the-cuff manner, "It just means that I look at the job and tell them how many men they need to do it efficiently." I have always loved the idea of having the perfect team in place to accomplish whatever task there was at hand.

As I look today, I realize that this is a human resources position. In fact, I discovered this handy definition: "Manpower management, which is also called human resource management, consists of putting a right number of people, the right kind of people at the right place, right time, doing the right things for which they are suited for the achievement of goals of the organization." This is the definition offered by a firm named Enormous Enterprises, which is a human resource provider.

As I read this definition, my heart swells with a desire that we would have enough help within the ranks of the local church to rightly determine the number and kind of people to employ in a particular area of need.

We mentioned the Pareto Principle earlier, which, according to Wikipedia, states that, "For many outcomes, roughly 80% of consequences come from 20% of causes (the "vital few"). Other names for this principle are the 80/20 rule, the law of the vital few, or the principle of factor sparsity." The Pareto principle applied to fundraising states that 80% of the funds come from 20% of the people, which we have witnessed to be true for the tithes of the church. It also states that 20% of the people do 80% of the work. We have also noted this to be true within the church.

This is such a factor that names have been given, such as "Cruise Ship Christians" (Jack Hibbs), or the satirical "potato family" allegory. It includes "Dick-tater" (he's just the boss), "Emmy-tater" (she's just a fake), "Hezy-tater" (he's just a stall), "Carmen-tater" (she has an opinion), "Agi-tater" (she's just trouble) and "Sweet- tater" (who happens to be the best of the bunch). Of course we can't forget "Speck-tater" … Speck's favorite phrase is: "I love work; I can watch others do it for hours." He doesn't get involved, but he's a great observer.

This is the persona that is out there concerning churches and Christians. It is appalling and shameful when you consider it. We are a family of slaves who have been freed by the sacrifice of the one who loved us and gave himself for us, and we can't seem to lend a hand so that everyone does a little.

I don't really believe it is necessary to list all the opportunities within the typical church to serve and to minister; rather, I think it begs the question, why?

Why are we willing to serve at the concession stand for the recreation league, but not in the food service at the church? Why are we willing to volunteer in our child's classroom at the school, but not in children's church once a month? Why are we willing to coach a child's team, but we are not willing to teach a child's class? What is it that keeps us from seeing the need at the church and then filling the need? How is it that we can build our own home gaming system and run our own online store, but we can't find the time to help with the audio/video ministry or the website at the church?

I am not sure what the correct answer is. It keeps me awake at times. How do we motivate? Why should we have to? Maybe we aren't clear enough about the needs of the church. Well, I am speaking to you right now, telling you without any doubt that your church needs your help. You have gifts and abilities that can benefit the church and will help get the message of the gospel to those who need it most.

What are you capable of that could bless your church? What will it take to get you involved in its ministry?

As for the aspect of being invested financially, I believe we have covered this well in our section on tithing. However, I will add that we should be as investment-minded at the Church as we are at the community center, the new school, the recreation center, the new community park and playground, etc. Just as we believe that there should be continual infrastructure and community improvement, we should be looking forward to the church as well. If we are willing to pay a little extra on the millage rate to get the park or the stadium for the high school, we should be just as willing to increase our giving at the church so that we can prepare for the next needed expansion of addition. If we are okay at the ballot box with a SPLOST (special local option sales tax) so we can get that new roundabout we need, then we should be okay at the tithing box with a SPLOT (special love offering today) for that new nursery we need. I am being a little facetious, but the point is we need to invest the money where it will have the greatest return on investment, and I don't know of anything that returns like eternal life.

We have discussed the need to be present, which is your attendance, attention, and affection. We have discussed the need to be available for ministry and management within the church and mission in the community. We have discussed the need to be invested both physically and financially. Now, lastly, we will consider the need to be resolute. What does it mean to be resolute? Notice this definition.

"Marked by firm determination: resolved, bold, steady."

A resolute person is not easily shaken, deterred, or distracted; they are determined and firm in their commitment. This is what your church needs. It needs you paired up and connected. It needs you to be present, available, invested, and resolute. Can we pray together?

Heavenly Father, thank you for saving my soul and making me whole. Father, I want to serve you, and I am convinced that the only way to do that is through the local church. Lord, I pray that You would forgive me for my failures and that You would bless me in this new commitment, this new resolve to be what my church needs me to be, as it fits in You and as it glorifies You. Amen.

Chapter Eleven
Habitual, Present, Attentive & Affectionate

My first inclination as I approached writing this final chapter was to just type the word "commitment" and be done. Indeed, that is what is required for you to become what your church needs.

And by commitment, I mean one simple commitment. I think so many folks make so many commitments that they are overwhelmed by the responsibilities of the commitments, and therefore, they are incapable of honoring the commitments. I also believe that people make "chain-linked" commitments, and if they are unable to honor one of them, then all of them fall. Lastly, (because I could talk about this all day) I am confident that people make commitments that are very hard to keep because they are entirely too ambiguous, such as "I will do better," "I will attend more," or "I will try harder." They are so non-specific there is no true accountability. After all, who can measure more, better, and harder? And against what are we measuring it? The pledge or commitment needs to be independent of other factors, it needs to be specifically defined, it needs to be known by someone other than yourself, and it needs to be readily attainable. This type of commitment will beget other, more significant commitments.

Although it would suit my personality, *which is kind of like a tall glass of sarcasm handed to you with a velvet glove, and followed by a warm hug*, to just write the word "commit" in several tenses, and utilizing all available synonyms, on several pages in redundancy; I am not at all sure that it would be profitable. So, we are going to take a stepped approach, but it will be brief.

There are three steps to becoming what your church needs you to be: first, you must know what your church needs; second, you must believe that the need is realistic; and lastly, you must commit to becoming what is needed.

In the previous chapters, I have attempted to define for you what your church needs; it is in the thesis statement. Your church needs *you*, sacrificially. The church needs your sacrificial involvement. I have attempted to phase the involvement by using words such as selflessness, service, and support so that a person could see the level of involvement needed. I have used my alliterative tools to aid in the mnemonic category. And yet I realize that there is no silver bullet, there is no perfect plea, there is no fool proof plan through which you will become a believer in the literal needs of the church.

You either recognize the Lordship of Christ, or you don't. You either realize the sovereignty of God, or you don't. You either believe the inerrancy of the scriptures, or you don't. In your mind, God is either the owner of everything or He is not. And lastly, you either comprehend the church as a literal body or you don't. That is the nature of such topics. They are learned in the illuminating light of the Holy Spirit; they are believed by faith (or not at all) because your eyes will certainly lie to you. Therefore, the Apostle Paul would say, "We walk by Faith and not by Sight."

So, there are some restraining factors. If you are a non-believer, then this is all nonsense to you. If you are a backslidden believer, the word backslide, in a Christian context, implies movement away from Christ rather than toward Him. A backslider is going the wrong way, spiritually. He is regressing rather than progressing. The backslider had at one time demonstrated a commitment to Christ or maintained a certain standard of behavior, but he has since reverted to old ways.

Backsliding may manifest itself in several ways, e.g., dropping out of church, losing fervor for the Lord, walking away from a ministry or a family, or falling back into old habits (definition according to GotQuestions.com). These things are all exaggerated to you. And if you are a non-conformist, these things are all institutional to you.

But if you are a born-again believer who is seeking the will of God in your life, you know these things are true and logical; they are reasonable. There is a yearning in your spirit, there is a nagging desire in your soul to please God. You are thinking, "These things may be true, but how can I change my entire schedule? How can I convert my entire mindset? How can I rearrange my whole budget?"

Cancel the hyperbole, stop the drama, and in the words of your high school principal, settle down now! It all starts with one commitment. Keep it simple, make it manageable, and make it known for accountability.

My commitment was simply this: "We will not miss any more church; if the doors are open, we will be here." I didn't promise to give up any habits, I didn't promise any money or giving plan, and I didn't even promise any participation because I didn't have mastery over any of those things. But I owned my schedule and could control how I invested my time, so I made the only commitment that I could make, and God honored it.

Who owns your schedule? Who owns your stuff? Who owns your family? Who owns your life? Who owns your heart? Who owns your eternity? Who owns your opinions? Who owns your allegiance? Who owns your dreams? Who owns your desires? Who owns your hopes?

Who owns you?

What does your church need?

It needs you – a sacrificial you.

How can you become what your church needs? Commit, pledge, promise, devote, commitment, konpromisoa, compromís, compromiso, komitmen, engagement, kudzipereka, comprometimento, kuzvipira kujitolea, engagemang, pangako, and most importantly commitment.

Heavenly Father, I come humbly and honestly thankful for all that you have given to me. My life, my family, my home, my career, and my possessions. I come, Lord, open handed and willing to give or receive as you see fit. I come committing myself to you and to your house; Lord please receive my commitment and help me as I seek to honor you through honoring it.

Appendix

Reasonable Church Membership Sermon Series

As I was writing this book the Lord allowed me to preach a three-week sermon series on the topic. The series title is "Reasonable Church Membership."

The series is very much in keeping with the thoughts expressed in this book. I used Romans 12:1, "I beseech you therefore, brethren, by the mercies of God, that ye present your bodies a living sacrifice, holy, acceptable unto God, which is your reasonable service," as my theme verse for the series, obviously setting the series title from the last phrase.

I have included my preaching outlines, which contain my notated commentary. These are obviously not the full transcripts of the sermons, but they are sufficient to understand the preaching impetus and possibly inspire of decision, I hope that you read them prayerfully and devotionally.

It is my earnest desire to see the Church whole, revived, and on mission. That means I desire that for every Bible preaching church in my city, because my city needs the Church. And I desire it for every Bible preaching church in my county, because my county needs the church. And I desire in for every Bible preaching church in my state, because my state needs the Church. And I desire it for every Bible preaching church in my corner of the country because the Bible belt definitely needs the Church, and I desire it for every Bible preaching church in my country, because America needs the Church. And I desire it for every Bible preaching church on this continent because all North America needs the Church. And I desire for every Bible preaching church in the cosmos, because the World needs the Church.

Reasonable Church Membership I

Unity, This Pastors Dream
Psalm 133:1-3

My goal, every time I preach is transparency. I always desire to tell you the truth. This morning I want to share, what I believe is God's design for the Church. Furthermore, I believe it is Satan's dread and defeat within the Church. And it is for certain this pastor's dream for the Church. It is quite simply unity. Unity among the brethren. And by unity, I mean a unified spirit of exaltation among the attendees, a unified spirit of edification in this Body, and a unified spirit of evangelization for this community. These are the ABCs of unity.

A church composed of unified brethren will be a prevailing church. A church composed of unified brethren will do a preserving work. And a church composed of unified brethren will be a productive effort.

This is Psalm 1 of the 15 Songs of Degrees. These Psalms begin with 120 and they conclude with Psalm 135. The thought behind the Song of Degrees is a classification also known as The Song of Ascents. According to Dr. John Phillips there is divided opinion as to what this means. *Some would say that they are "A song of the higher choir" or "In a higher key" It may have to do with the stages of return back to the promised Land after the captivity, or it may be prophetic referring to the final in gathering of the Jews, some have suggested that it is related to the restoration of the ark to Jerusalem, and of course many believe they are relative to the fifteen steps of Ezekiel's temple.* Regardless, Psalm 133 is one of the 15.

William MacDonald outlines this Psalm with four main points – It is good and pleasant when brothers dwell together. It is fragrant. It is refreshing. And finally, it is a sure guarantee of God's blessings. We could certainly use this suggested outline, and indeed we will not stray far but notice with me.

I. The Defining qualities of Unity

I have already mentioned the characteristics of a unified church. That is prevailing; as against the gates of hell, and preserving; as in salt that preserves, and productive; as in fruit bearing. The question is can we rightly associate this Psalm and the contents and encouragement therein with the Church?

I believe the short answer is yes, and I am in good company as many commentaries would agree. You will notice that the unity that is being described is among the *brethren*! These brethren, in order to be brethren must share parentage. They are, in this passage, Jews, God's chosen people.

Well according to the New Covenant you and I, if we are born again, are in Christ, and therefore we are the sons of God, for as many as are led by the spirit of God, they are the sons of God. The spirit itself bears witness with our spirit, that we are the children of God: and if children, then heirs, heirs of God, and joint heirs with Christ. We are brethren in the family of God. And this Psalm is of immense value and application to the Church!

Notice the simplistic terms that the Psalmist uses to define the qualities of the unified brethren, first he states that:

A. *Unity of the brethren is Good* – There is an inherent value found in the unity of the brethren. It is beneficial. Unity breeds solidarity, and solidarity strength, and strength ability. Indeed, the

Church is described in multiple passages as a body. Many members one Body. A whole body fitly joined together and compacted by that which every joint supplies, according to the effectual working in the measure of every part. Even if other issues arise, even in difficulty, even in tribulation, the unity in and of itself bears an inherent value. *It is Good!*

B. *Unity of the brethren is Pleasant* – We also note that it is pleasant. It is good and pleasant. It is pleasing, it is agreeable.

C. It is satisfying. It is joyous. It is desirable. And it is attractive, something to be reached for, something to be pursued.

Notice the penman never says that unity is guaranteed, he doesn't say that unity is easy, he doesn't say that unity is simple, he doesn't say that unity is automatic. He doesn't even say the unity is promised. But unity is good and pleasant.

I wonder today, this morning if all hearts and minds were laid bare would we see unity? Would we witness a network of unified dreams, and desires for our church and community? Would we see pleasing lines of parallel personal preferences all bowing to the undeniable need for Christ in our community and in our county, state, and country? Or would we see individualism and division? *Notice next.*

II. The Details concerning Unity.

I am considering the question, "How can we practice unity?" I notice in the details concerning unity that we see two requirements. Notice first that:

A. ***Unity is expressed in Dwelling*** – This is the verb attached to unity in this particular verse. We must dwell in unity. That is we must remain. We must abide. We must tarry. We must stick around. We must hold on. We have to be here. This could easily be applied to attendance. I realize many may not be thrilled with that application and it is certainly not the absolute application, but we must be honest enough with one another to realize that if we are to experience unity it is going to require some level of faithfulness and dependability. I am certain there are many well-meaning, born again, church members who rarely experience that good pleasantry of the unity of the brethren which results in strength and solidarity simply because they cannot find a stability of attendance. *Notice the modifier, or the condition of the dwelling.*

B. ***Unity is marked by Togetherness*** – You will not experience unity by dwelling separately. The qualifier for unity is togetherness. When we, as the Body of Christ, come together, in one spirit, for one cause, unto one end, and we dwell together in that work we experience the goodness of unity! We must settle down into the work, together, with the strength and solidarity to complete that work we are then expressing unity and we can begin to experience.

III. The Desirable effects of Unity

The Psalmist gives two examples of the blessings of unity. Both are indicative of the anointing presence of the blessed Holy Spirit. First, he mentions the anointing of Aaron with the special oil. Then he mentions the dew that falls on Hermon and Zion. Both are types of the

A. *Anointing of the Spirit which brings:*

- *The sweet aroma of God – the oil*
- *The sustaining blessings of God – dew*
- *The sacred peace of God – peaceful life*
- *The shared promise of God – eternal life*

In Leviticus as the Aaronic Priesthood was established, Moses would pour that anointing oil, which was a holy oil, a type and/or picture of the Holy Spirit of God, unique, and devoted, a work of the perfumer and a recipe meant to be used only for the work of the temple and the priesthood! This oil would signify the blessing of God, the consecration unto holiness, and it would emit the sweet aroma of the perfumer.

Likewise as we dwell together in unity, we will experience the sweet aroma that comes from the indwelling Spirit of God, the blessings of His presence, the identification that comes from the pouring out of the spirit, the inclusion that comes from the baptism of the spirit into the Body of Christ, and the insight that comes from knowing that we belong, many members, one Body, one spirit, called in one hope of calling, one Lord, one faith, one baptism, one God and father of all, who is above all, and through all, and in us all.

And then there is the example of the dew that would fall from Hermon and descend all the way to Zion. That is a continual blessing, a covering blessing, a consummate blessing of the Lord upon all the Land of Israel. This speaks to the sustaining blessing of the indwelling Holy spirit of God. If the Oil represents the Identification, the Inclusion, and the Insight of the anointing of God then the dew would illustrate the increase that He brings as we are covered in the anointing of the spirit and we begin to be fruitful, refreshed again and again by the blessings of God. And the blessings are innumerable in that they are sufficient for all who belong.

Lastly, we see that these blessings result in life for evermore. We can view this is two ways, first we would consider how that as the Apostle Paul states that we were dead in trespasses and sin, but that He quickened us. We are crucified with Him, yet we live, not we ourselves but Christ lives within us, and the life that we now live in the flesh we live by the faith of the Son of God who loved us and gave His life for us! Life evermore!

We may also see that we are the conduit through which this life evermore may find its way to a lost and dying world. We have been given the words of life and we can share them or stuff them under our hat. We can preach them, practice them, project them with our lives or we can pervert them, and turn them into a parody of truth, or wisdom which will only offer a parody of life evermore. What are these words of Life.

They are the gospel, the eternally settled truth of the word of God.

That are all descended from Adam, we are all fallen in sin, conceived in iniquity, and born in sin. We are destined for condemnation, but God so loved the world that he gave His only begotten Son, that whosoever believeth in Him should not perish but have everlasting life. This is life evermore.

Reasonable Church Membership II

Last week I spoke on "Unity, the Pastors Dream." It was the first of a three-sermon series entitled "Reasonable Church Membership." This week I plan to speak on "Body Position, the Members Place." And next week "Calling, the Members Responsibility."

My thoughts are centered around one phrase or clause, in one verse of one passage. That passage is very common, and oft quoted. It is Romans 12:1, "I beseech you therefore, brethren, by the mercies of God, that ye present your bodies a living sacrifice, holy, acceptable unto God, which is your reasonable service." The clause that I am concerned with is at the end of the verse. "Which is your reasonable service," you may also read it as, "Which is your spiritual worship," or "Which is your spiritual service of worship." The word used in this phrase as "reasonable" is the Greek word "logikos." In general, we see the idea of logical, reasonable, sensible, or rational. Meaning that based upon the work of Christ and the gift of salvation, it would seem to be reasonable, logical, sensible, to offer your body as a living sacrifice. Or you might prefer this thought, "based upon the mercies of God, the mercy He has shown in offering His only begotten Son as your substitute, you should live your life in such a way that it resembles a living sacrifice unto God. This only reasonable, it is only logical, it makes sense." Or, and lastly you may better understand in this way. "Since God, by His mercy, has provided you with resurrected life, by the substitutionary death of His Son, you should live as a sacrifice unto Him which is performed in and through your spiritual service."

And then The Apostle Paul would continue in Romans 12 to discuss the Body, and the members place therein. He also discusses the individual members attitude concerning themselves (wherein he states that they should not think more highly of themselves than is right), he deals with how we interact with one another, and he deals with unity as well in verse 16. So, we are certainly within the context of the church. Now let's consider;

Body Position – The Members Place
1 Corinthians 12:12-27

I am confident that you have heard of the Body. The Body of Christ. The Church Body. The Church as the Bride of Christ again suggesting that we are a body, the Body of the Bride. Christ, the head of the Body. This metaphor is used profusely to attempt to describe the living organism that consist of all the born-again believers from Pentecost to today, and until the rapture or the catching away of the Church. That is the Church. If you are born again, you are a part of that church, you are a part of that living organism, you are a part of that Body of believers.

The Apostle Paul uses this terminology in several passages. He speaks of the Body in his letter to the Romans, again in His letter to the Corinthians, again in His letter to the Ephesians, and again in His letter to the Colossians. He carries that metaphor to a spectacular exhibit in the passage that we are considering today. Notice first as we consider that.

I. The Body owns a Holy Designation – Organism
vs. 12-14 and vs. 27

Here in these verses Paul makes it clear that the Church is one Body, and that the one Body is Christ. There are many of us, but when we are born again, and the Holy Spirit takes up residence us, we are then immersed (baptized – *baptizo*) into the Body with all the other born again, spirit filled believers. Our nationality doesn't matter, our privilege or lack thereof doesn't matter, our background doesn't matter, the only thing that matters is that we are filled with the Spirit of God, which is the case for every born-again believer! So, the initial entry into the Church is worry free, stress free, it is not a chore, or a work, it is a grace benefit provided by the Spirit of God, if you are born again, you are a member of the Body of Christ.

We understand this contextually because He is writing to the Church at Corinth! And He states in verse 27, "Ye *are* the Body of Christ," the fact of it and the fundamental truth of this are not a mystery because it is plainly stated. Now the function of it, the spiritual understanding of it may be a mystery but like many other truths we are taught concerning things of faith, we must reckon this to be so and live in light of it.

As is relative to the church this means that the individual Christian must not only comprehend that he or she is a member of the Body – that is a functioning, necessary part of the Body, but they must also then conduct themselves in like manner.

We will notice in a moment that if the believer ignores this responsibility or if they halfheartedly attend to this responsibility the remainder of the Body will suffer the consequence of that inaction. But it in no way relieves that believer of the responsibility, and the need remains in the Body. We will discuss this more in a moment. But if you stopped for a moment and considered yourself. Could you say that you are a born-again believer? If so, do you realize that you occupy a place in the Body? And if so, are you functioning within the Body, the living organism of the Church? *Note next.*

II. The Body offers a Habitat for Diversity – vs. 15-20

In verses 15-16 we begin to see some of the human element of this membership. What if I become self-conscious about my given position in the body. What if I decide that I am unhappy with my particular membership? What if I decide that I don't care for my position. Or I decide that I no longer want to participate? Can I just refuse, can I just withdraw, can I just determine that I am no longer a part of the Body?

Interestingly enough it looks like the answer to that is no. Paul says just because a member determines to no longer be a part of the Body, it is still attached to the Body. When you consider this in the physical sense, your hand has no authority over itself, your eye has no authority over itself, and so on. This could be encouragingly considered considering eternal security... I think for the purpose of this sermon the more interesting value of this passage is that idea of diverse abilities and functions. There is so much room for individuality within the Body, and yet individualism can be cancerous. We can be ourselves, in the way God made us, exercising the gifts and unique personalities given but we must remember that those things were given for corporate blessings, edifications, encouragements, and they were given to the glory of God. Rather than being for the glory of the flesh, or for the exaltation of man, or the expression of self. We must contend with that part of our nature that makes us seek our own above others. And it is quite difficult, and it is ongoing, and it can be exasperating! I want to say, once again, that I believe you can neglect your body position but there will be a need, a want, a void in that area because God has designed it for you to do it. Ephesians 2:10, "For we are his workmanship, created in Christ Jesus unto good works, which God hath before ordained that we should walk in them."

Again, will you take an honest look at yourself right now? Have you considered what your diverse gift is? How could it be used within the Body of Christ? When you exercise your diversity is it to the glory of God and for the good of the Body? Or is just you, being you because that's who you are, how you are, the way God made you, and folk just need to get used to it or get over it? The Body is a habitat for diversity but not a home for division.

III. The Body offers a Harmony of Dependence – vs 20-24

In verse 24 Paul uses the phrase "tempered the body together" the Greek there literally means to mix-together. You might read the word composed, mingled, harmonized, or combined. I really like the KJV use of the word tempered, which can be defined as, "to dilute, qualify, or soften by the addition or influence of something else." That's what should happen in the Body of Christ, all these gifts and abilities, personalities and preferences come together, united by the Holy Spirit of God, and suddenly we have an elite team assembled for victory.

The thought is that we need one another. We need these various differing personalities and abilities to fill the need in the community within which God has placed the local assembly that we are involved. And the eye cannot flippantly disregard, or discard the hand, simply because the hand cannot refract light. What if you were placed on a high platform and instructed to hold on with your eyes! Also, the inward parts should not be castigated because they are soft and mushy, oh the liver is gross, oh the kidneys are gross and mushy, and wet, and bloody and they're not very tough... You know what happens if you don't have a liver? You die... You know what happens if you don't have a kidney? You die...We need each other, because we are designed by God to fulfill a specific role and that role cannot be effectively, or efficiently filled by anyone else.

All the aspects of the physical body have a metaphorical application to the Church Body. All of them, health, exercise, diet, hydration, rest, amputation, disease, phantom pain etc. Lastly note.

IV. The Body offers a Hedge of Dedication – vs. 25-26

We are accustomed to speaking about a hedge of protection, which is there as well, but in this passage, we see that there should be no schism, no division, only devotion and dedication unto one another as is fit for the body! Loving one another. Caring for one another. Suffering together. Celebrating each other. That is what a Body does, every member, every organ working together for the health of the whole! This is the need in the Church.

As a final question, are you dependent and dedicated to the Body? Or are you perfectly comfortable outside of and away from the Body? If you are comfortable away from the Body, how would you explain that comfort in light of this passage?

Reasonable Church Membership III

CALLING, THE MEMBERS RESPONSIBILITY
EPHESIANS 4:1-16 - (Romans 12 – 1Corinthians 12)

We have been discussing "Reasonable Church Membership" for the past two weeks, this sermon will conclude that conversation. We have used Romans 12:1 as our thesis or impetus for this series as it states therein that Being a living sacrifice unto the Lord *is* our "reasonable service."

The Apostle Paul was quite concerned with the issues of church membership and participation. Naturally his idea of church membership was grounded in our relationship to Christ rather than a particular local assembly, but he was writing to local assemblies. And in most cases, he spoke of Body health, participation, and function, so much so, that I believe we can equate active attendance, and participation within the local assembly to a healthy walk in Christ. In fact as Paul opens the fourth chapter of the book of Ephesians in which he will discuss body position, health, and responsibility he offers the imperative that we should "walk worthy of the vocation which we are called," and he goes on to define that walk as one of humility, and meekness, endurance, and patience in love; to the end that we would keep the unity of the Spirit through the binding power of peace.

And in order to safeguard against being misquoted or misunderstood allow me to invert the application. If you have a healthy relationship with Christ, it will be reflected in a healthy and active participation in the local assembly. However, if you are basing your eternal security upon your work(s) within the local assembly you have put the cart before the horse. The attendance, and participation within the Body of Christ are reflexive rather than restorative. You can be a great church member and still be in need of a savior, but once you have been born again a healthy walk will be reflected in your active, faithful attendance and participation within the Church.

We have considered unity, and unity is paramount to the success of the Church accomplishing its mission. Last week we discussed Body Position and the simple fact that if you are a born-again believer you occupy a position within the Body of Christ and there is a need for you to perform the functions of that position. This week we will look at our calling within the Body and we will consider our responsibility. *Notice first.*

I. The Veracity of universal Gifting
Ephesians 4:7 & Romans 12:3
"Every Born-again Believer has a Gift – or more."

This speaks directly to the false idea that some are gifted, and others are not. Notice the phraseology, "Unto every one of us" in Ephesians 4:7, we would compare this with Romans 12:3, "For I say, through the grace given unto me, to every man that is among you, not to think of himself more highly than he ought to think; but to think soberly, according as God hath dealt to every man the measure of faith." Again, we see the inclusive terminology of "every man" or better stated "everyone."

There are no invalids in the family of God unless they have chosen to be invalids. Everyone is gifted, everyone is given certain gifts and abilities. And if we consider the Parable of the Talents, and/or the Parable of the Minas, we will even believe that a proper investment of your gifts and abilities would lead to an increase in gifts and abilities. Remember the statement, "You've been faithful over a few things, I will give you charge over many things." Also consider the statement, "Unto whom much is given, much is expected."

So, we are met with the thought that all are gifted; by someone, in some way, for some particular purpose. No one can claim disability in the Lord's house. No one can claim inability in the Body of Christ. No one can claim to be useless or unwanted in the Body of Christ. When indeed you were born with natural gifts and abilities. You were born with diverse gifts and abilities. And then. If you are saved, you were born again, and indwelt with the Spirit of God, baptized into the Body of Christ, and gifted at that time with a spiritual gift. So, you have your natural gifts and abilities that would likely be beneficial to the Body of Christ, and you have whatever spiritual gifting that God has granted based upon your body position. So that the question shifts from gifts and abilities to obedience and willingness. Are you willing? Are you obedient? *Next note.*

II. The Valid origin of the Gifts – Eph.4:7-11a & 1 Cor. 12:4-6
"All gifts come from the same place, same person, same Spirit!"

We see in the Ephesians passage that Paul states these gifts are gifts of Christ. He quotes from Psalm 68:18 concerning how He, that is the Messiah, would give gifts to men, and he concludes his statement with the first three words of verse 11, "and He gave."

Then if we consider the passage in 1 Corinthians we notice, "different gifts but the same spirit," in verse 4 and then in verse 5 we read, "different administrations but the same Lord," and then lastly in verse 6 we read, "different operations but the same God which worketh in all."

There is no doubt as to the origin, or the source of the gifts. They all *come from God*, they are all *administered by the Lord,* and they are all *given by the blessed Holy Spirit.* No one gift is more special than the other, no one ability carries any greater blessing than the other. The spirit *enlists* them all, the Lord *employs* them all, and God is *exalted* in them all. The Body needs them all, it is *sensitive* to them all, it is *served* by them all, and it is *strengthened* by them all.

And therefore, the Mission of the Church is s*ubject* to them all! Are you employed by the Lord, within the Body, and unto the Mission of the Church? *Consider next.*

III. The Variety of potential Gifts – Romans 12:6-8
"The types of gifts are innumerable, but there's one for every need!"

As we consider the Ephesians passage, we see the offices of apostles, prophets, evangelists, pastors, and teachers and I think folks read this and they see specific callings that possibly they have not received and then they believe that maybe others are absolved from any regular, detailed service within the Body of Christ. But that is simply not the case.

Paul states that these particular callings are placed and then those who are called are gifted to the Church for the perfecting of the saints, for the work of the ministry, for the edifying of the of the Body of Christ. This is better stated in the ESV, "to equip the saints for the work of ministry, for building up the body of Christ." So, what is the work of the ministry? Isn't that what we are discussing? Aren't we stating that a healthy Christian walk will result in the regular, active, participation in the local assembly?

Look at the passage in Romans and we see a different list, we see words like ministry (service), teaching, exhortation, giving, ruling (leadership), diligence, mercy, love, clinging to good(righteousness), kindness, honor, fervency, rejoicing in hope, patience in tribulation, distributing to the necessity of saints, and hospitality. We could probably sum up or encapsulate all of the needs of the local body of Christ in this one list.

When we merge these two passages, we see that the pastors, and evangelist, and teachers are sent to the Church in order to train and equip the body, the members to accomplish these things within the Body.

And we see that the gifts are as varied as personalities. That means that you likely possess (everyone is gifted) a gift or an ability, or a personality trait that can be refined through the preaching and teaching of God's word and applied to the health of the body to help the Church accomplish its mission. And it brings us back to the question of willingness and obedience. *Lastly note.*

IV. The Vital purpose of the Gifts – Ephesians 4:12-16
"All gifts are given to Glorify God, and to Witness unto Christ!"

The purpose is, as we have already stated, to mature the believer. To build up or strengthen the Body. To further the unity of the family of God. To ground the believer in the truth and doctrine of the inerrant Word of God. And to establish the Body in love.

Christ would say to His disciples, A new commandment I give unto you, that ye love one another; as I have loved you, that ye also love one another. By this shall all men know that ye are my disciples, if ye have love one to another. And I am saying to you that when we are faithful to the Body we will be established in love and others will know that we are His disciples.

And then the Lord said to the disciples in Acts as he prepared to ascend "You shall be witnesses unto me! This is the purpose of the Church. To glorify God and to be witnesses unto Christ. Therefore, gifts are given, and the end unto which they should be expressed. It is to establish the church so that the church may exercise its responsibility and evangelize the community unto which it is sent.

Do you know Jesus as your Lord and Savior?

What is your gifting?

In what way could you serve the Body?

About the Author

Cory Sexton pastors Hoschton Baptist Church in Hoschton, Georgia, where he's served in leadership since 2012. He oversaw a decade of significant growth for the church, including the purchase of a 30-acre property and multiple building projects.

Cory attributes the success and impetus behind Your Church Needs You to the selfless, sacrificial commitment of the many lay members who call Hoschton their home church. In 2023 he created a Scriptural and ethical framework for church engagement called Heroic Church Membership, which he turned into a sermon series. An eponymous book version soon followed.

Cory regularly speaks to like-minded audiences, challenging them to rise up and answer the needs of their local churches. He's been married to his wife, Karla, for 33 years, and together they have two children — Kayla, 30, and Carter, 25. In his spare time, Cory enjoys hunting, football and spending time with his family.

Milton Keynes UK
Ingram Content Group UK Ltd.
UKHW020914180424
441376UK00013B/397